Don't Think, Smile!

Don't Think,

Ellen Willis

Smile!

Notes on a decade
of denial

Beacon Press
Boston

Beacon Press
25 Beacon Street
Boston, Massachusetts 02108–2892
www.beacon.org

Beacon Press books
are published under the auspices of
the Unitarian Universalist Association of Congregations

05 04 03 02 01 00 99   8 7 6 5 4 3 2 1

An earlier version of "The Majoritarian Fallacy" appeared as "We Need a
Radical Left" in *The Nation*, June 29, 1998.

Portions of "Decade of Denial" were first published in the *Village Voice*,
the *Boston Globe*, the *New York Times Book Review*, *Salmagundi*, and *Newsday*,
in articles that appeared between 1992 and 1998.

An earlier version of "Race and the Ordeal of Liberal Optimism" appeared as
"The Up and Up" in *Transition* #74, December 1998.

"Beyond Good and Evil" first appeared in *Tikkun*, May/June 1994.

"Freedom, Power, and Speech" first appeared as "Porn Free" in *Transition* #63,
Summer 1994.

"Intellectual Work in the Culture of Austerity" was first published in *Post-
Work*, edited by Stanley Aronowitz and Jonathan Cutler, Routledge 1997.

"Their Libertarianism — and Ours" first appeared in *Dissent*, Fall 1997.

This book is printed on recycled acid-free paper that contains at least
20 percent postconsumer waste and meets the uncoated paper
ANSI/NISO specifications for permanence as revised in 1992.

Text design by John Kane
Composition by Wilsted & Taylor Publishing Services

Library of Congress Cataloging-in-Publication Data
Willis, Ellen.
        Don't think, smile! : notes on a decade of denial / Ellen Willis.
            p.   cm.
        ISBN 0-8070-4320-6 (cloth)
            1. Libertarianism.   2. Radicalism.
    JC585.W55   1999
    323.44 – DC21   98-47264

For Nona

CONTENTS

The Majoritarian Fallacy

When Ronald Reagan was elected in 1980, a wide assortment of liberals and leftists called for unity around a campaign for economic justice. Since then, as the country has moved steadily rightward, I have heard this call repeated countless times, along with many hopeful announcements of projects designed to put it into practice. Each time the right wins an egregious victory (as in the congressional elections of 1994), dozens of lefty commentators rush into print with some version of this proposal as if it were a daring new idea. Recently, the editors of the *Nation,* kicking off a series of articles for which writers had been invited to contribute their thoughts on restarting a stalled movement, once again lamented the left's failure "to unite around economic issues of fairness that join together the interests of all but the wealthiest Americans." You would think that if economic majoritarianism were really a winning strategy, sometime in the past eighteen years it would have caught on, at least a little. Why has it had no effect whatsoever? Are people stupid, or what?

The culprit the majoritarians seem to have settled on is cultural politics. The cultural left, they argue, has given left politics as such a bad name because of its divisive obsession with race and sex, its arcane "elitist" battles over curriculum, its penchant for pointy-headed social theory, and its aversion to the socially and sexually conservative values most Americans uphold. As a result, the right has been able to distract American workers with the culture war, while pursuing class war with impunity. Some anticulturalists further claim that cultural radicalism is the politics of an economic elite that itself has a stake in diverting the public from the subject of class to, as Michael Lind put it, "inflammatory but marginal issues like abortion." It's true that the cultural left, with its middle-class origins, has too often been guilty of class bias and incognizance of class issues. But note the elitist, condescending assumptions embodied in the majoritarians' arguments: that for two decades most Americans have been manipulated into abandoning their true interests for a cultural sideshow; that they don't have the brains to tell one kind of leftist from another, let alone come up with their own ideas about what kind of politics might improve their condition.

I'd suggest a different explanation for the majoritarians' failure: their conception of how movements work and their view of the left as a zero-sum game—we can do class or culture, but not both—are simply wrong. People's working lives, their sexual and domestic lives, their moral values are intertwined. Capitalism is not only an economic system but a pervasive social and ideological force: in its present phase, it is promoting a culture of compulsive work, social Darwinism, contempt for "useless" artistic and intellectual pursuits, rejection of the very concept of public goods, and corporate "efficiency" as the model for every social activity from education to medicine. In every sphere, Americans face the question of whether they will act, individually and collectively, in behalf of their own desires and interests, or allow established authority to decree what they must do, what they may not do, what they deserve, what they have a right to expect. If they do not feel entitled to demand freedom and equality in their personal and social relations, they will not fight for freedom and equality in their economic relations. Furthermore, people are not "distracted" by the moral and cultural issues that affect their daily existence as much as the size of their paychecks; they care passionately about those issues. The right owes much of its success to the fact that it speaks to this passion, while the left is largely indifferent, ambivalent, or ready to embrace whatever the polls say is popular.

In any case, class is itself a cultural as well as economic issue. The idea that a heterogeneous population is naturally inclined to band together on the basis of its declining share of income relative to the rich makes sense only on the same bonehead premise advanced by conservative "rational choice" theorists: that human beings are economic calculating machines. In fact, a powerful ideology of meritocracy divides people of different socioeconomic strata as effectively as (and usually in combination with) racism or sexism. While large percentages of the working and middle classes may tell pollsters they think CEOs make too much, on a deeper level most people tend to admire the rich, to see them as somehow smarter or better, just as they tend to despise the very poor. In the '90s, tycoons like Bill Gates have emerged as culture heroes, up there with multimillionaire entertainers and athletes. Peoples' identities are bound up with their sense of superiority to those below them on the class ladder and their vicarious identification with those above, as well as with the values, language, styles, and habits associated with their particular niche in the social order. To argue for a solidarity that transcends such social divisions and demystifies "success" is already to challenge deeply ingrained cultural patterns.

Indeed, class-based movements are no less susceptible than those grounded in race or sex to the temptations of "identity politics"—that is, politics based on the belief that the worth of an idea or cultural practice should be judged not by its substance but by the group identity or social standpoint of its proponents. Much of what passes for pro-working-class politics is primarily aimed not at abolishing (or even mitigating) class distinctions, but rather at defending "working-class values"; *ressentiment* against the "cultural elite" takes precedence over making alliances with middle-class intellectuals, feminists, and so on, which would require some respect for the latter's concerns. This is why blue-collar unions have been reluctant to organize white-collar workers, and why in certain circles preference for beer and pretzels over wine and cheese has been elevated to a political badge of honor. Similarly, populism, which is regularly invoked as a model by the majoritarians, is at bottom a form of identity politics or cultural nationalism for so-called ordinary people. Populism and "workerism," like other variants of nationalism, define membership in a political community through the exclusion of others and defend the received values of that community against outsiders. Such movements equate collective values with dominant values, denying conflict and punishing dissidence within their own ranks.

Majoritarian leftists have rightly criticized the grip of identity politics on the thinking of the cultural movements. More dubiously, they habitually conflate cultural radicalism with identity politics, ignoring its universalist, libertarian roots (racial and sexual liberation movements are not ultimately about group interests but about human freedom and equality, while radical critiques of the family and work are not based on "identity" at all). Yet ironically, the majoritarians themselves are strongly drawn to the identity politics of class. The perceived conflict between class and cultural politics arises not because they are intrinsically incompatible but because majoritarian leftists have uncritically equated the cultural values of workers and "ordinary people" with their historically dominant voices: white, straight, male, and morally conservative. Besides contradicting the Enlightenment universalism the majoritarians supposedly advocate, this view is increasingly out of date. Thanks to the impact of the '60s, the dominant culture of Middle America and its working class is no longer so monolithic, if in fact it ever was. The majoritarian left is still bedeviled by the image of hard-hat construction workers and their outraged contempt for antiwar demonstrators; but for me that image is eclipsed by the reality of the working-class Vietnam vets I met while I was helping to run a movement center near Fort Carson, Colorado: men who vociferously opposed the war, who smoked the same dope, listened to the same music, and grew the same wild hair as the draft resisters. Now, of course, there is the reality of a public that refused to be shocked by the Starr Report or to support Bill Clinton's impeachment.

Left reluctance to credit the reality of the past forty years is exemplified by a comment of *Nation* columnist Eric Alterman's, made in response to some letters criticizing an article in which he had opposed the economic-justice left to "the racism/sexism/homophobia crowd." "I did not and would never argue that race and gender are not important — indeed critical — areas of analysis," Alterman writes. "But politically, in this country, they appear to be losers. Class-based leftists have the New Deal to pose as a model of twentieth-century reform. Where is the analogous model of successful coalition-building and progressive legislation for would-be identity politicians?" Leaving aside the reductive "identity politician" label, this is a rather breathtaking dismissal of the changes wrought by the black, feminist, and gay movements in every area of American life, from our sexual mores and our popular culture to the once taken-for-granted racial caste system and rigid masculine and feminine roles enforced by law and custom. In fact, the victories of these movements, along with

those of environmentalists, stand as the left's major achievement since World War II. As for the New Deal model, progress
along those lines ground to a halt in the '70s, and nothing
"class-based leftists" have done since has been able to arrest
the steady disintegration of the liberal state or the triumph of
free-market ideology. By Alterman's standards, this record
would suggest that class politics is a loser for the left. Fortu-
nately, it's only the majoritarians' version that warrants this
judgment.

The project of organizing a democratic political movement
necessarily entails the hope that one's ideas and beliefs are
not merely idiosyncratic but speak to vital human needs, interests, and desires, and therefore will be persuasive to many
and ultimately most people. But this is a very different matter
from deciding to put forward only those ideas presumed
(accurately or not) to be compatible with what most people
already believe. No mass left-wing movement has ever been
built on a majoritarian strategy. On the contrary, every such
movement—socialism, populism, labor, civil rights, feminism, gay rights, ecology—has begun with a visionary minority whose ideas were at first decried as impractical, ridiculous,
crazy, dangerous, and/or immoral. By definition, the conventional wisdom of the day is widely accepted, continually reit-
erated, and regarded not as ideology but as reality itself. Rebelling against "reality," even when its limitations are clearly
perceived, is always difficult. It means deciding that things
can be different and ought to be different; that your own
perceptions are right and the experts and authorities wrong;
that your discontent is legitimate and not merely evidence of
selfishness, failure, or refusal to grow up. Recognizing that
"reality" is not inevitable makes it more painful; subversive
thoughts provoke the urge to subversive action. But such
action has consequences—rebels risk losing their jobs, fail-

ing in school, incurring the wrath of parents and spouses, suffering social ostracism. Often vociferous conservatism is sheer defensiveness: people are afraid to be suckers, to get their hopes up, to rethink their hard-won adjustments, to be branded bad or crazy.

It's not surprising, then, that those who stick their necks out to start social movements tend to be in certain respects atypical. Paradoxically, they are likely to have economic and social privileges that free them from an overwhelming pre-occupation with survival, that make them feel less vulner-able and more entitled (in the labor movement, for instance, skilled workers have usually been first to organize). Or con-versely, they may already be social outcasts or misfits in one way or another and so feel they have little to lose. Often they have been exposed to alternative worldviews through a radi-cal parent or an education that encouraged critical thinking. Such differences are always invoked to attack radicals on the grounds that they are not "ordinary people" but middle-class intellectuals, cultural elitists, narcissists, weirdos, outside ag-itators. Yet rebellious minorities are really just canaries in the mine. When their complaints speak to widespread, if unad-mitted, disappointments and desires, it's amazing how fast ordinary people's minds and the whole social atmosphere can change, as happened between the '50s and the '60s.

My experience as an early women's liberation activist was dramatic in this regard. At first we were a small and lonely bunch; our claim that heterosexual relations were unequal everywhere from the office to the kitchen to the bedroom was greeted with incredulity, laughter, and blunt aspersions on our sexual and emotional balance. I had many passionate arguments with women who insisted they loved to cook and cater to men. What was I doing, they demanded—trying to destroy sex and love? Two years later feminist groups were erupting all over the country, and it was not unusual to see women turn up at demonstrations who had once denounced the whole enterprise in the most withering terms. Suppose we had reacted to that first wave of hostility (as of course many liberal feminists urged us to do, and many liberal men no doubt wish we had) by concluding, "This will never fly—let's stick to 'equal pay for equal work' "?

It's not necessary, as many leftists imagine, to round up popular support before anything can be done; on the contrary, the actions of a relatively few troublemakers can lead to popular support. The history of movements is crowded with acts of defiance by individuals and small groups—from the 1937 sit-in of workers in a Flint, Michigan, auto plant, to Rosa Parks's refusal to get up, to radical feminists' disrupting an "expert hearing" on abortion reform—that inspired a wave of similar actions and a broader revolt. When militant minorities also have radical ideas, they capture people's imaginations by presenting another possible world that appeals to the secret hopes even of the resigned and cynical. They mobilize people by providing the context in which winning small changes is worth the time and effort because it is part of a larger project. They attract publicity and make it difficult for the authorities to keep on telling the lies whose credibility depends on uncontradicted repetition. The people in power know all this and are quite wary of the potential threat posed by an organized minority; their impulse is to make concessions (albeit as few as they can get away with). As a result, radical movements that articulate a compelling vision have an impact far beyond their core of committed activists.

American left politics, when successful, has generally worked this way: as radical ideas gain currency beyond their original advocates, they mutate into multiple forms. Groups representing different class, racial, ethnic, political, and cultural constituencies respond to the new movement with vary-ing degrees of support or criticism and end up adapting its ideas to their own agendas. With these modifications, the movement's popularity spreads, putting pressure on existing power relations. Liberal reformers then mediate the process of dilution, containment, and "co-optation" whereby radical ideas that won't go away are incorporated into the system through new laws, policies, and court decisions. The essential dynamic here is a good cop/bad cop routine in which the lib-erals dismiss the radicals as impractical sectarian extremists, promote their own "responsible" proposals as an alternative, and take the credit for whatever change results.

The good news is that this process does bring about sig-nificant change. The bad news is that by denying the legiti-macy of radicalism it misleads people about how change takes place, rewrites history, and obliterates memory. It also leaves people sadly unprepared for the inevitable backlash. Once the radicals who were a real threat to the existing order have been marginalized, the right sees its opportunity to fight back. Conservatives in their turn become the insurgent mi-nority, winning support by appealing to the still potent in-fluence of the old "reality," decrying the tensions and disrup-tions that accompany social change, and promoting their own vision of prosperity and social order. Instead of seriously con-testing their ideas, liberals try to placate them and cut deals, which only incites them to push further. Desperate to avoid isolation, the liberal left keeps retreating, moving its goal post toward the center, where "ordinary people" supposedly re-side; but as yesterday's center becomes today's left, the entire debate shifts to the right. And in the end, despite all their ef-forts to stay "relevant," the liberals are themselves hopelessly marginalized. This has been our sorry situation since 1994.

Now, in the wake of the impeachment debacle, the right is

in disarray and the left has a chance to regain the offensive. But the moment will be lost, and the left continue to lose ground, unless it gives up the untenable distinction between economics and culture to which it is so stubbornly attached. Majoritarianism is a means of denying this reality and maintaining the distinction without having to defend it on its merits. Some majoritarians are cultural conservatives who are sympathetic to much of the right's pro-family, work-without-end program but don't want to be attacked for saying so. Others are satisfied with the cultural status quo—okay, it's not perfect, but hey, what is?—and are baffled and irritated that these "marginal issues" should steal attention, as they see it, from what matters to *them*. (In this vein, Richard Rorty has lectured *Nation* readers, "Let's stop airing these doubts about our country and our culture"—in other words, *have* your damn doubts, but don't frighten the horses. Apparently he has decided, like former speaker of the House Tom Foley on the occasion of the 1989 American invasion of Panama, that "this is not the time for a lot of complicated debate.") Still others have concluded that in light of past crimes committed in the name of utopia, raising the possibility of social transformation is simply too dangerous.

Cultural radicalism *is* dangerous. It weakens established institutions while offering no guarantees that new social forms will work and many opportunities for terrible blunders. Worse, it attracts authoritarians bent on perverting its liberatory aims into canons of "correct" thinking and behavior: too many participants in contemporary cultural politics have indeed learned all too little from the grim history of the totalitarian left. But the alternative to engaging in the risky business of trying to build a genuinely radical social movement is inability to confront the power of global capital and right-wing authoritarianism in any meaningful way. And such paralysis is not just dangerous: it is the route to certain disaster.

The essays in this book are grounded in the conviction that a democratic, libertarian radicalism is possible, as well as necessary. In expressing this conviction, I am speaking for myself, not for "the American people," as the majoritarians purport to do. Yet the weight of my experience leads me to suspect that in my desire for a freer, saner, and more pleasurable way of life, I am not so different from most people, American or otherwise, as it might presently appear. It is this hopeful suspicion that keeps me writing.

Don't Think, Smile!

I

Decade of Denial

Don't Think — Smile!

High on my list of petty urban irritations are those signs posted by smug possessors of driveways: "Don't Even *Think* about Parking Here." I fantasize about plastering their premises with superglued bumper stickers that say "Down with the Thought Police" or "Don't Even *Think* about Telling Me What to Think." It occurs to me, though, that the signs are an apt metaphor for the one-way conversation carried on by driveway guards who call themselves journalists: "Don't even *think* about questioning the need to balance the federal budget." "Don't even *think* about workers getting a fair share of the wealth they produce." "Don't even *think* about the problems with the institution of marriage that punishing unmarried mothers won't solve."

Commentators are always inviting me to accept as a foregone conclusion conservative dogma on some issue I had foolishly imagined was debatable. Consider the *Wall Street Journal*'s obituary of Barry Goldwater, which assures the reader, "Today even liberal Democrats agree that some part of Social Security should be privatized." Or the Manhattan Institute's James Pinkerton, opining in *Newsday* about the high rate "among some groups" of unmarried childbearing, "leading, everyone now agrees, to the chaos and crime of the urban underclass." Or the *New York Times*'s classic "News Analysis" of the 1996 budget battle: the president, the reporter remarked, was disinclined to move because "he now can make the argument that Democrats . . . are the defenders of education and the elderly while all the Republicans care about is tax cuts. It is a flawed argument, especially on Medicare, for Mr. Clinton knows as well as the Republicans do that spending on such entitlements must be curbed eventually." Not "Mr. Clinton *believes*," which is undoubtedly true, but "Mr. Clinton *knows*." Don't even *think* about the government raising revenue for social spending by restoring the progressive income tax, or making steep cuts in the post–cold war military budget. If you're the kind of crank who has to have irrational doubts about what everybody *knows*, go join the Flat Earth Society.

For the past few years, everybody has known that we are enjoying a terrific economy, with out-of-sight stock and real estate prices, jobs going begging, even the wages of bottom-tier jobs beginning to creep up. Never mind that the statistics don't measure involuntary part-time and temporary employment, or the steady flow of people (especially people over fifty) out of jobs with good pay and benefits to those offering neither, or the conversion of real jobs to sub–minimum wage "workfare" slots; that a minority has garnered most of the wealth, while real estate inflation has displaced all but the rich and the subsidized from boom towns like Manhattan; that the current growth rate depends on an unstable mountain of debt. Meanwhile, much of the world economy is in crisis. Sooner or later, Roadrunner will figure out that he's treading air, and Americans will rediscover their enduring reality: growing economic insecurity, a long-term decline in real wages, and fewer social benefits and public services. No doubt the gatekeepers of our collective wisdom will revert to their usual strategy of convincing people there's nothing much to be done about these miseries other than blaming themselves for not striking it rich as everyone else seems to have done, or blowing off steam at corrupt politicians, the undeserving poor, the immoral cultural elite, the unqualified blacks who are supposedly getting all the good jobs, and so on.

But there's a problem looming: call it the euphoria gap. If you can't get with the most marvelous expansion since the '6os, you're a sorehead. But when the bubble sags, your discontent will once again be worrisome to what might be called the "conservative center"—that is, the financial and corporate establishment, the "new Democrats," those Republicans whose antiliberal zeal stops somewhere short of radical right-wing anarchism or militant Christianity, and their countless flacks in the think tanks and mass media. For the CC, it's not enough that Americans "know" they have no choice but to accept a declining standard of living; it's essential that they accept this adversity with good grace. The ultra-right traffics in anger, which it hopes to enlist in behalf of its vision of counterrevolutionary change. But the CC wants to control the pace of change, and understands that popular anger is a wild card. While its main priority is avoiding a class revolt from the left, it is also leery of all-out culture war from the right: congressmen in league with white supremacist militias, or worse, Pat Buchanan, covering both bases with his rabble-rousing populism, nationalism, and fundamentalism, are a conservative centrist's nightmare. How then to get us to chill out?

I'd suggest reissuing Robert J. Samuelson's *The Good Life and Its Discontents: The American Dream in the Age of Entitlement, 1945–1995*. It was published in 1996, while memories of the right's government shutdown were still fresh and before the boom hype had taken hold, to enthusiastic reviews in the *New York Times* and the *Wall Street Journal. Newsweek* ran an excerpt as a cover story: "Cheer Up, America! It's Not as Bad as You Think." Americans are unhappy, Samuelson argues, not because we're really doing badly, but because we're hooked on unrealistic expectations. The post–World War II economic boom led us to envision a utopian future of ever rising incomes, stable jobs, personal freedom and fulfillment, and government solutions to all social problems. But the boom ended, and conditions reverted to what we ought to accept as normal but experience as betrayal and disillusionment. It's time to pull up our socks, relinquish our overweening sense of entitlement, and settle maturely for what we've got.

Samuelson has a point about the naïveté of American optimism. The extraordinary affluence of the postwar years and the liberal social compact that allowed most people to share it were the product of a unique set of circumstances. Not only did the United States emerge from World War II an economic superpower, but business, labor, and government were resolved, in the wake of depression and war, to save capitalism both from its own tendency to crisis and from the socialist threat represented most concretely by the Soviet Union. The translation of phenomenal economic growth into high wages, job security, and social benefits was a formula for buying people's loyalty to the system, neutralizing potential radicalism, making genuine economic equality seem unnecessary. For capitalists, who relinquished some of their profits but never their power, collaboration with labor and the welfare state was strictly a temporary marriage of convenience. For most Americans, it was a historical shortcut to the pursuit of happiness. As with our abuse of the environment in the name of growth, and our abuse of antibiotics in the quest to "conquer disease," the bill for that complacency is now coming due.

This, however, is not exactly the point Samuelson wants to make. For him, capitalism is a given, a natural fact. The economy is like "a vast river, where fish and plants flourish and perish and where occasional floods occur." Its inherent "instability, insecurity, and excess" may be hard to take, but without it we wouldn't have computers and microwave ovens. So absolute is Samuelson's assumption that there's no possible alternative to this system that he doesn't even bother to say so. (I mean, didn't the fall of Communism lay that one to rest forever? Don't even *think* about it.) During the '6os, when this now taboo subject was actually raised in public, defenders of capitalism used to argue that despite its inequities, it delivered the goods. Now they're reduced to arguing that you can't control a river. But what's happened to the economy over the past two decades has nothing to do with laws of nature; it's the product of conscious and deliberate social policy.

Prodded by competition from Europe and Japan, American capital invested in cheap third world labor markets and job-decimating technologies that undermined American workers' bargaining power; unconstrained by a left grown pitifully weak, business abrogated the liberal compact. Employers embarked on a concerted campaign to break the unions (which don't get even a token mention in Samuelson's account of the "forces" behind shrinking wages). Government obligingly deregulated, threw out progressive taxation, declared the austerity state, and is now taking an ax to those programs that represent the last vestige of the idea that markets ought to be subordinate to the needs of society, not vice versa. As computers allow companies to produce more and more with fewer and fewer workers, so that profits and stock prices go up with every round of layoffs, productivity is being decoupled from income as surely as sex from procreation. Yet the idea of plowing back some of the wealth generated in the process into support for the unemployed is sacrilege to the free-market ideologues who run the country. River? What we've got here is a steamroller.

There's a strong element of déjà vu in Samuelson's "Party's over, get used to it" message. The first concerted assault on "the age of entitlement" took place in the '70s, the decade of the energy crunch, the New York fiscal crisis, and the first wave of "pro-family" activism; it was the theme of the Carter administration. Then the strategy was moral intimidation: our greedy profligacy had led government to overspend; our narcissism (women's especially) had undermined the family; we were a bunch of lazy, morally flabby slobs who had better shape up. The main result of all this guilt-tripping was that Americans elected Ronald Reagan, who reassured the electorate that material aspirations were fine so long as they were channeled into private gain, and that it wasn't the American people who were lazy, morally flabby, and narcissistic, just feminists, gays, blacks, and welfare queens.

But by now, conservative centrists know better than to lecture people about tightening their belts when they're already doing so, willy-nilly. Instead Samuelson offers economic determinism: prosperity made us do it. It's not our selfish desires we must curb, but our overstimulated imaginations. Don't worry—it only hurts when you think.

Candide in the Global Village

On the occasion of its fiftieth anniversary in 1995, the neoconservative flagship journal *Commentary* devoted its pages to a symposium on "The National Prospect." Nearly all the respondents—mostly a Who's Who of the right, though a few stray centrists and left social conservatives were included—were optimistic about our country's future, hopeful that conservatives really were, after all that wandering in the desert, on the up side of history. Indeed, several contributors invoked the prospect of a new Great Awakening. There was much talk of the need to combat the lingering legacy of the '60s, those myriad subversions of morality, religion, and social cohesion perpetrated by villains ranging (in *Commentary* associate editor Gabriel Schoenfeld's inimitable rhetoric) "from the multiculturalists loose in our schools to the murderers loose in our streets." There was somewhat less talk about economics, most of it complacent, though a few contributors did worry about inequality and others were concerned that economic libertarianism, taken too far, would encourage the social libertinism they deplored.

Taking this all too familiar tour, I began to experience an odd sense of unreality: no one was talking about the elephant in the room. I refer to the question that has to be the starting point for any serious assessment of the national prospect— namely, how is the unprecedented reach and momentum of global capitalism going to affect the very idea of the nation-state, and with it American identity? This issue lurked behind all the others the editors had asked the symposium participants to address, from immigration to the possibility of common American values. What did it mean that a panel of conservative luminaries from all wings of the movement could simply ignore it?

To begin with, the ascendancy of global capital has confronted conservatives with an uncomfortable choice between their loyalty to the American nation and their loyalty to the free market. The people who control transnational corporations and the world financial markets may be citizens of one country or another, but in their capacity as investors and conduits for wealth, they have no a priori stake in any country's well-being. Before the fall of Communism, they had a political interest in America as the mainstay of anti-Communism around the world; even now the American government is still too politically and militarily powerful to entirely disregard. Nonetheless, America for the transnationals is basically a market and an influence on other markets, and their chief concern is access to those markets on the most favorable possible terms. If the American middle class ends up collapsing as a result of their disinvestment in a labor market deemed too expensive — well, tomorrow to fresh woods and pastures new.

The power of corporations to invest or disinvest, to lend or refuse to lend, amounts to the power to manipulate and ultimately to control public policy. That can mean investing in the campaigns of politicians who do their bidding or disinvesting in a country like Sweden that tries to hold on to its welfare state; withholding loans to former Communist countries that don't move fast enough toward privatization or threatening to lower New York City's credit rating if it raises taxes. Such decisions are made every day and, like most of what "the market" does, are usually taken for granted, as if corporate investment priorities, like capitalism itself, were a natural fact, like the weather. American conservatives' success in weakening the federal government and starving it of funds will not lead to a democratic dispersal of power to local governments closer to the people; it will merely accelerate the process of consolidating corporate economic power on the transnational level. What can "American democracy" mean when no one even bothers to hide the fact that economic policy is made, not by elected officials accountable to their constituencies, but by the croupiers of global capital's floating crap game?

To complicate matters, the conservative resurgence itself owes a good deal to the rise of globalism. The social contract between business, labor, and government that post–World War II liberalism represented — the contract that ruled during the period that's the object of so much conservative nostalgia—depended on the existence of an American business class committed to national prosperity and stability. When business reneged on that commitment, liberals could no longer deliver, and the resulting economic anxiety has done much to drive the cultural reaction that proponents of traditional values would prefer to attribute to Americans' simply recovering their common sense. If the anxiety gets worse, however, conservatives are likely to get a lot more than they bargained for—a mass radical right-wing movement.

The loyalty problem has led some conservatives (none of them contributors to the symposium) to advocate subordinating free-market ideology to economic nationalism, whether in Pat Buchanan's populist/nativist version or in forms more akin to liberal statism. On a world scale, militant nationalism has followed economic globalism as surely as it once followed colonialism; but while it has served as an outlet for strong and deadly emotions, it has never solved the economic and social problems that provoked it. Of course, the United States isn't Bosnia, or even Russia. A determined, popularly supported economic nationalism might work for us for a while, since the croupiers can't yet afford to blow off America as easily as New York. But finally this is a losing game. No nation-state, however strong, can permanently withstand an economic colossus that knows no borders. In the end, just as Ronald Reagan was willing to decimate the air traffic control system to show the strikers who was boss, world capital would take its money and run—despite the costs and dangers of doing so—to break an American rebellion. In short, nation-states are on their way out as the world's chief means of organizing political and economic power. What does this do to our national prospect? Does the idea of a national prospect even make sense?

It would be grossly unfair, of course, to claim that the right has a monopoly on obtuseness about these questions. To dispel any such sectarian illusion, I have only to imagine the contents of a similar symposium in an organ of the left like the *Nation* or *Dissent*. In recent years a long line of commentators—from liberals like Arthur Schlesinger Jr. and Richard Rorty to former new leftist Todd Gitlin to populists Michael Tomasky and Michael Kazin—have insisted that two principles are basic to a left revival in this country. First, the proper aim of left politics is mobilizing liberal democratic government to promote economic justice: it is not our business to try to change the culture or politicize relationships that belong in the realm of "civil society." Second, the left must repudiate the "politics of difference" and subordinate racial, sexual, and other particularist identities to our common identity as Americans, which is founded on the ideal of liberal democratic government. In other words, we are to hitch our movement to a state whose power is rapidly eroding, an identity inseparable from that state, and an economic goal no state is in a position to achieve.

Like conservatives, and for not so different reasons, these writers look fondly back on the heyday of liberal nationalism. I could argue with various aspects of their fondness, but in truth the argument is moot, since the conditions that sustained the welfare state, or what we new left types used to call corporate liberalism, no longer exist. In recent years, the left has aggressively forgotten how little the New Deal and the postwar standard of living had to do with the virtues of liberal democratic government, and how much with what business felt compelled to do in response to popular social movements and Soviet competition. Nor has it really grasped the import of the appalling irony that defines the post–cold war era. By showing that another system was not only possible but able to compete for world dominance, the tyrannical Soviet regime forced Western capitalists to adopt more humane policies, while its unlamented demise has spurred the triumphant and vengeful resurgence of nineteenth-century laissez-faire, on a grander scale than was ever imaginable before. Which is to say that the viability of American liberal democracy was in some sense dependent on the subjugation of Russia and Eastern Europe—and undone by the liberal revolutions of 1989. That a solid American identity may soon melt into air does not mean that common American experiences, sensibilities, political ideals, and cultural values don't exist, or that they will simply crumble into the old dustbin. If anything, given the global ubiquity of America's material and ideological influence, "Americanness" is peculiarly suited to floating away from its moorings in the nation-state and adapting itself to the contours of a postnational world. To begin with, the American talent for constant reinvention should be especially useful in a time when the state is coming apart and the meaning of politics is up for grabs. In fact, reinventing politics is exactly what Americans have been doing: the cultural radicalism anathematized by the Rortys and Gitlins has been, among other things, an effort to apply certain basic American democratic values—freedom, equality, the right to pursue happiness—to the institutions of civil society and the social relations of everyday life. Not coincidentally, the impact of the American cultural left has traveled far beyond U.S. borders.

In some ways too, the American multicultural and feminist impulses that both the right and much of the left see as "balkanizing" are anticipating the devolution of the state by looking elsewhere for commonalities—with Eastern European women, say, or a worldwide African diaspora. Economic inequality—which is also balkanizing, after all—may have a similar effect. As the great majority of Americans come to have more in common with their working-class and middle-class counterparts in other countries and less and less with the putatively American wing of a global ruling class—and as it becomes increasingly chimerical to define American identity by a sense of entitlement to a middle-class standard of living, with any exception regarded as the individual's bad management or bad luck—it also becomes more likely that Americans will begin looking past national boundaries for class-based alliances.

But who would have thought the state would start withering away and the left wouldn't even notice?

Hamlet in the Global Village

In itself, the war in Bosnia was an extraordinarily brutal and devastating event; as a disastrous exercise in politics by other means, its impact is only beginning to be felt. The success of the Serbs' genocidal campaign to impose ethnic separatism in the Balkans and to savage the very idea of democratic, cosmopolitan modernity, European complicity in their project and American reluctance to oppose it—these central themes of the Bosnian story have nothing but the most unsavory implications for the future of the West, Eastern Europe, and the world. Already the predictable next chapter is at hand, as Slobodan Milosevic pursues his ferocious campaign of "ethnic cleansing" in Kosovo.

Of all the wrenching questions raised by these events, none is more revealing of the state of the American left than the one posed by Susan Sontag in a *Nation* article as germane today as when it appeared in 1995. "No one," Sontag wrote, "can plead ignorance of the atrocities that have taken place in Bosnia. . . . And no one can be unaware that the Bosnian cause is that of Europe: democracy, and a society composed of citizens, not of the members of a tribe. Why haven't these atrocities, these values, aroused a more potent response? Why have hardly any intellectuals of stature and visibility rallied to denounce the Bosnian genocide and defend the Bosnian cause? . . . The writers, theater people, artists, professors, scientists who have a record of speaking up on important public events and issues of conscience . . . have been as conspicuous by their absence from the Bosnian conflict as they were by their presence in Spain in the 1930s."

This quiescence, Sontag supposes, can in part be attributed to widespread anti-Muslim prejudice and "heartless historical cliches" about the "eternal conflict" and "implacable ancient rivalries" that afflict the Balkans. But there is also the fact that "this is not the 1930s. Not the 1960s." Rather, this is an age that no longer provides clearly defined targets—fascism, Communism, imperialism; an age in which "the final victory of capitalism, and of the ideology of consumerism . . . entails the discrediting of 'the political' as such. All that makes sense is private life." In such an atmosphere, Sontag charges, Western intellectuals have been depoliticized, have become cynical and selfish, focused on their own private pleasure and convenience. At best, they can be mobilized for "limited actions—against, say, racism or censorship—within their own countries. . . . There has been a vertiginous decay of the very notion of international solidarity."

Confronted with this angry indictment, I'm immediately tempted to proffer a list of counterexamples—articles, conferences, symposia, teach-ins, open letters, advertisements. Yet it's indisputably true that Bosnia inspired no outpouring of public indignation from American or European intellectuals comparable to that surrounding the Spanish Civil War or Vietnam. Even worse—if one takes seriously the idea that a society ought to be able to look to its intellectuals to analyze and interpret events, to examine them in a larger historical and political context—in the United States at least (I don't know about Europe), there has been far too little discussion of the war that goes beyond superficial, platitudinous hand-wringing on the one hand and realpolitikal noodling about strategic options on the other.

As Sontag recognizes, this gap in our public conversation has everything to do with the devolution of politics that has been gathering terrifying speed since 1989. Intellectuals' public embrace of a political issue doesn't come out of no-where; it reflects a social climate in which a critical mass of people, particularly in the universities and the media, have a sense of urgency about politics in general and the feeling that what they say or do can make a difference. Such a climate, in turn, depends on the existence of movements and organizations already primed to anticipate the eruption and inter-pret the significance of national and international crises. More specifically, the proliferation of passionate pro-Bosnian voices that might have made a difference was unlikely to emerge in the absence of an active radical democratic left. (Al-though individual conservative intellectuals have supported the Bosnians and condemned "ethnic cleansing," the right in general has no passion for democracy or cosmopolitanism, except insofar as they open up markets, and no real objection to ethnic separatism, except insofar as it challenges white power.)

Although Sontag—who at the time her piece appeared had been to Sarajevo nine times and devoted considerable energy to publicizing the Bosnians' plight—has earned the right to chastise her peers, ultimately I think her emphasis on their personal morality is misplaced. No doubt complacency, cynicism, distaste for inconvenient entanglements have be-come increasingly commonplace among American intellec-tuals, as more generally in the upper middle class to which most intellectuals belong. But Sontag might have considered another, less venal if equally problematic side of left intellec-tuals' flight into privatism—their frustration, depression, and demoralized withdrawal in response to an ascendant right's relentless consignment of leftism of any sort to the political margins. Certainly, intellectuals these days seem far less inclined to solipsistic hedonism than to joylessness and puritanical absorption in work. And if they are more inclined to rise to the discrete domestic issue than the historic international moment, this may have less to do with the decay of the notion of international solidarity than with the decay of confidence in their ability to change the world, not to mention the decay of anything resembling a coherent framework of ideas within which to understand it.

What remains is a set of vestigial attitudes, carried over from a time when the left did have some impact on international affairs, that are less than helpful for understanding an event like the Bosnian crisis or organizing a response to it. Although the idea of American imperialism no longer explains much in a world where the locus of power is rapidly shifting to transnational corporations, it still fuels a strain of reflexive anti-interventionist sentiment whose practical result is paralyzed dithering in the face of genocide. Floating around "progressive" circles and reinforcing the dithering is a brand of vulgar pacifism whose defining characteristic is not principled rejection of violence but squeamish aversion to dealing with it. In the academy in particular, entrenched assumptions about identity politics and cultural relativism promote a view of the Balkan conflict as too complicated and ambiguous to allow for choosing sides: if there is no such thing as universality, if multiethnic democracy has no more intrinsic human value than ethnic tribalism, if there are no clear-cut aggressors and victims—merely clashing cultures—perhaps ethnic partition is simply the most practical way of resolving those "implacable ancient rivalries."

These blindnesses and confusions are bad enough. But the muted response to the horrific cruelty of the war also suggests that some kind of active repression is at work. I'd guess that many people resist coming to terms with the meaning of Bosnia because an honest assessment would involve questioning a cherished axiom of post-1989 common sense — namely, that the breakup of the Soviet Union and Yugoslavia into small independent states was self-evidently a good thing, a necessary and proper step on the road to East European democracy, the expression of a sacred "right to national self-determination." On the contrary, I'm convinced, the people of former Yugoslavia, the Bosnians most of all, would be infinitely better off if they had stayed together in a federation.

"Ancient hatreds" did not destroy that possibility; mundanely modern political interests did. It was Western Europe that stood to benefit from the fragmentation of a potentially powerful neighbor; Western capitalists who had a stake in the breakup and the cultivation of nationalist competition as insurance against any flare-up of egalitarian notions carried over from the Communist past; demagogues who saw their opportunity and moved into the breach. To define the war simply as good, democratic, multiethnic nationalism versus the bad racist, fascist kind — while a big improvement over defining it as the unfortunate consequence of ineluctable Balkan enmities — stops short of getting to the root of the problem, which is nationalism itself. This too is a problem that the American left, still deeply attached to the idea of national liberation and national governments, has yet to face.

Left Out

The morning after, November 1994: a dirty job, but somebody had to do it — assess the left's reaction to the congressional putsch. My problem, however, was finding a left to assess, at a time when conventional notions of the political spectrum were shifting to the right with a speed reminiscent of German hyperinflation in the '20s. One went to bed assuming Bob Dole was a bona fide member of the hard right, and woke up to find he'd become a moderate. Bill Clinton, on the basis of his feeble lurch toward health care reform, had been branded the next thing to a Marxist revolutionary, while the modest social liberalism that was one of his selling points in 1992 (and that he had been backing away from ever since) was equated with the ultimate in radfemqueerthink. The Democratic Leadership Council was hectoring him to "move toward the center," occupied, presumably, by Newt Gingrich. On Black Tuesday (though who knew what Wednesday might bring), it seemed that a leftist could be defined as anyone who didn't want to repeal the income tax, thought public schools were a good idea, and doubted that putting poor kids in orphanages was the solution to welfare dependency.

This ideological bracket-creep lent a certain absurdity to the right's determination to interpret the election results as an omnibus revolt against New Deal liberalism and '60s cultural radicalism. So enthusiastically did conservatives push this line that both the *Wall Street Journal* and the *New York Post* enlisted me in its behalf, quoting a comment I'd made in the *Village Voice* that the Clintons were "inescapably '60s figures." In fact, I was making precisely the opposite point—that Clinton's frantic attempts to distance himself from his image as a "counterculture McGovernik" (Gingrich's phrase) and his socially liberal impulses had, if anything, increased his political enemies' contempt, while confirming most people's impression that there was no there there. The 1994 election was not a repudiation of the left—you can't repudiate something that for all practical purposes doesn't exist. Rather, it demonstrated that the electorate abhors a vacuum.

By then the list of Americans' frustrations was long and growing: economic insecurity, overwork or not enough work or stultifying, regimented work at insultingly low wages, with no prospect of improvement and no margin for illness or retirement; recognition that the dream was over, that education and hard work guaranteed no reward whatsoever; crime, lousy schools, disintegrating public services, lack of community, racial and ethnic tension, conflict between the sexes, familial instability, no time for personal life and child rearing. All this had exacerbated people's sense of government as an alien institution that took their money for purposes decreed by arrogant bureaucrats and corrupt politicians, was impervious to their influence, and did nothing to address their problems.

The right put these grievances in the context of its own vision; it offered an analysis, a set of principles, a program. While much has been made of the divisions among Republicans—economic libertarians versus religious rightists, internationalists versus isolationists—from 1980 through the early Clinton years they subordinated their disagreements to a coherent overall message. Politically, they identified the cause of our problems as a government that neglects its primary duty to maintain law and order, discourages enterprise by taxing and regulating business, destroys individual freedom and opportunity by promoting special rights for groups, and confiscates the hard-earned money of productive citizens to support an out-of-control debt, a huge bureaucracy, and a parasitic, immoral, dangerous underclass. Culturally, they blamed the '6os—shorthand for the decline of traditional religious and moral authority, the demand for personal freedom and social equality, the revolt of blacks, women, and gays, the sexual revolution, the normalization of divorce and single parenthood.

In response, the "left" (see definition above) offered neither a competing vision of the good society nor an alternative analysis of our ills nor a believable strategy for tackling them.

Its main activity was directing moral appeals for justice and compassion to a Clinton administration and a Democratic Party that paid it as much attention as a buzzing fly. On the cultural legacy of the '60s, leftists were divided. But few were willing to defend its radical libertarianism—as opposed to liberal platitudes about inclusion and diversity, or the authoritarian moralism that so often passes for militance on behalf of the oppressed—while the hostile and dismissive voices steadily increased in both number and volume. A significant portion of the left had always been uncomfortable with cultural politics, especially feminism and gay liberation. In the '70s, as the social atmosphere grew more repressive, many leftists, liberals, and even feminists decided that the politic course was to back away from any controversial criticism of traditional moral, sexual, and familial values, while some urged that the left court Middle America by actively embracing cultural conservatism. With the triumph of Ronald Reagan, a beleaguered, defensive, and thoroughly deradicalized left (which had taken to calling itself "progressive," a word that aptly conveys the righteous vagueness of the politics it describes) generated an outpouring of sentiment on behalf of the old-time economistic religion. In the interest of uniting to oppose the massive upward redistribution of wealth—so the line went—divisive social issues must be downplayed if not ignored altogether. And anyway, wasn't it time to admit that the defenders of work, family, and virtue had a point?

Some of us sharply disagreed. We argued that "progressives" who allowed the right's moral agenda to go unchallenged—thereby tacitly supporting its demand that people submit to authority and stifle their desires for freedom and personal fulfillment—could not expect to be taken seriously when they urged people to stand up to authority as embodied in the formidable alliance of corporate CEOs, public officials, economists, educators, and all manner of "experts" who had decreed that the new economic order, like it or not, was a permanent and non-negotiable fact of life. You could make a good case that the ensuing years, in which the corporate juggernaut rolled over abject unions and a quiescent public, more than validated this point of view. By 1994, you could also point out that the left's only recent claim (pathetic as it was) to making a dent in national politics had been electing a president who exuded the whiff (faint as it was) of sex, drugs, rock and roll, Vietnam, and feminism, amid widespread alarm about the Christian right's attacks on working women, single mothers, and gays at the 1992 Republican convention. But apparently neither fourteen years of almost unrelieved defeat nor the exception of Clinton's candidacy had inspired any second thoughts in the progressive camp.

As for the Democrats, from the start of the Reagan era they had responded to the conservative challenge in two characteristic ways: defending the status quo—mainstream social liberalism, the shrinking welfare state—or (increasingly) me-tooing the right on both fronts. Since most Americans were desperate for some kind of change and much preferred passionate conviction to half-hearted, opportunistic pandering, both Democratic strategies were basically losers. When Democrats won, it was usually because the ultra-right got carried away with itself and refused to temper its rhetoric with reassuring nods to tolerance and democracy. That had happened in 1992; it would happen again in 1996, after self-styled congressional "revolutionaries" shut down the government rather than compromise with the president on the budget. Nineteen ninety-four, on the other hand, presented the classic and predictable case of a party with energy and ideas smashing a sclerotic, demoralized operation that had nothing whatsoever to say. And if this event turned out to be the defining political moment of the decade—a moment that not only shaped national policy for the next four years, but set a tone that made it thinkable to impeach the president for illicit sex—it is largely because the opposition, such as it was, stubbornly refused to smell the coffee.

Was *anyone* out there, in the wake of the tsunami, countering the right's unleash capitalism–return to morality–get the poor off our backs offensive with a convincing alternative? Not so far as I could tell. As I made my dispirited way through the putatively leftist postmortems, the first thing that struck me was their unselfconscious similarity—references to current events and issues aside—to the postelection commentary of 1980. Once again the common theme was a call for economic populism, with or without an explicit invocation of New Deal liberalism (i.e., liberalism before 1968, when all those nasty social issues came along). While most of these proposals simply ignored cultural issues, or argued that an appeal to class would defuse them, some defined cultural conservatism as an integral part of the populism the left should embrace. In *Newsweek*, Joe Klein argued, "There *was* a subtle alliance between 'left-wing elitists' and the nascent black underclass in matters of personal morality in the 1960's." In the *New York Post*, Jack Newfield appealed to "fellow Democrats" to "Dump Bill": "Liberals ought to stand for traditional values like work, family, law, discipline, patriotism and individual moral responsibility."

Back at my home base, the *Voice*, our postelection cover was devoted to Michael Tomasky proclaiming, "Tuesday's returns were the final referendum on a left-liberal agenda that paid too much attention to its tiny narcissisms and too little attention to the needs of most Americans." "Narcissism," for any feminist or gay liberationist who had experienced the first round of cultural backlash in the '70s, was a fighting word. As popularized by the late Christopher Lasch's *The Culture of Narcissism*, it had been regularly invoked against those of us who argued that real radicalism was about affirming the right to freedom and pleasure, unmasking the repressive functions of institutions like Family and Work. But in the grim context of the '90s, this sort of narcissism, tiny or huge, was rarer than steak tartare.

That the left's problem was not an excess of self-love but a paucity of ideas was amply demonstrated by Tomasky's brand of belligerently anti-intellectual populism. "Most Americans," as he saw it, work, pay taxes, have children, want the trash picked up, go to school so they can get a secure job so they can "own a home and do the regular things Americans . . . want to do," and "think Fish and Jameson stand for a dinner of carp and Irish whiskey." Whereas the "liberal elites," who presumably don't work, pay taxes, have kids, or believe in garbage collection, and are off doing perverted rather than regular things, "sit around debating the canon at a handful of elite universities." Never mind that Tomasky's portrait of Average Joe was as condescending as anything the "liberal elites" could dream up. (In fact, the apathy about class that is indeed all too common on the academic cultural left is the flip side of this know-nothingism.) Even more telling was his assumption that academic debates were inherently trivial. Conservatives, in contrast, knew that it mattered what went on in universities, especially the elite kind. Decisions about what got taught there—what counted as bona fide knowledge— resonated through the educational system and the culture as a whole, which is why the right, *not* the left, had made changes in the canon and other aspects of academic culture a major public issue.

Tomasky did make one statement with which I entirely agreed: "There's no surer way to create new generations of conservatives . . . than to let the right take the lead on welfare, crime, immigration. . . . The left isn't offering [people] an alternative way of doing things that makes any sense in their lives." Exactly! And what might that alternative be? In a follow-up piece, he spelled it out: the left should combine a progressive economic program with a rethinking of the "categories of left and right" on social issues. Education, for instance: "Why is it wrong for the left to advocate higher learning standards, a longer school day, a longer school year?"

"Higher learning standards"—who could disagree? But what that meant was not as self-evident as Tomasky seemed to think. Conservatives had strong ideas about what should be taught, how, and to whom. They liked old-fashioned authoritarian pedagogy, indoctrination in morals, official inspirational versions of history, great books for the elite, vocational training for the masses. There were radical alternatives to this agenda, but developing and presenting them entailed the kind of discussion Tomasky would no doubt dismiss as elitist thumb sucking, on the grounds that Average Joe thought Dewey was Donald Duck's nephew. As for a longer school day and year, why should the left uncritically embrace this nose-to-the-grindstoneism, which also demanded that adults work longer and longer hours? My daughter, then in the fifth grade, had school six hours a day (less twenty minutes for lunch) plus homework time, ten months a year. Why wasn't that enough? What was wrong with having the time to play, to relax in hot weather?

Then there was welfare: "The left resisted welfare reform for years. Some of the left even argued, years ago, in favor of expanding welfare rights. ... Well, those arguments were lost. The welfare laws are going to be rewritten. The point is to write them in a humane way." Aside from its Orwellian flavor—how do you "humanely" pretend there's a job at a living wage out there for any welfare recipient who tries hard enough, or "humanely" punish women for having children outside marriage?—this pronouncement suggested that there were only two positions you could take on welfare: defend the existing system or accept the assumption behind the present reform campaign, that people are poor because they are lazy or immoral. Yet '60s new leftists had criticized the welfare system as a means of pacifying and controlling poor people instead of attacking economic inequality. And given the economic and technological changes eliminating "good jobs" at an accelerating rate, it might be time to stop thinking in terms of relief for a discrete class of "the poor" and discuss what a universal guaranteed income might look like. If you wanted to talk about genuine left alternatives, those were good places to start. If, on the other hand, you were simply tired of losing and eager to come in from the cold, Tomasky's "If you can't beat 'em, join 'em" approach definitely had the edge.

While the message was familiar, on closer inspection there *was* something new about the way its 1994 version was being delivered—a note of angry aggrievement. Tomasky made explicit what the anger implied: rather than merely urging cultural leftists to back off and get with the program, he actually blamed them for the ascendancy of the right. This would be a recurring theme in the writings of progressives in the latter half of the '90s, in books like Todd Gitlin's *The Twilight of Common Dreams*, Richard Rorty's *Achieving Our Country*, nouveau liberal Michael Lind's *The Next American Nation*, and Tomasky's own entry, *Left for Dead*, as well as numerous polemics in the *Nation* and elsewhere.

It seems that a bunch of academics, tiny as their narcissisms may be, have nonetheless managed to take up all possible space left of center, leaving the people they turn off with no choice but to throw in their lot with the Republicans. But how is this possible, given that the left opponents of cultural politics have hardly been silent all these years? Why is the public not listening to the cultural left's progressive critics? If they are so much more in tune with the concerns of ordinary people, why do they have so little political influence, either as an independent voice or as a faction of the Democrats? Socially conservative leftists have long complained that it's in the interest of the elite that runs the Democratic Party and dominates the media to promote cultural liberation rather than class issues. But this charge can't explain why the right has been so much better at grassroots organizing than the economic-justice left, or (the same question, really) why the Democratic Party elite has not felt the need to appease its economic progressives the way the Republican elite (often to the detriment of its own class interests) has appeased its social reactionaries.

It's hard to avoid the conclusion that disgruntled liberals and leftists have projected onto the cultural left their own deep sense of failure—and furthermore that the real reason for their anger is not the supposed irrelevance of cultural radicalism but, on the contrary, its enormous and lasting impact. The '6os liberation movements may have sprung largely from the middle class "liberal elite," but their influence ultimately spread through all social strata: no American has been untouched by the changes in sexual mores and male-female relations, the breakdown of taboos on public expression, the demand for a cleaner environment and a healthier diet, the new centrality of paid work to women's lives, the increasing racial and ethnic heterogeneity of mainstream American life. Nor have three decades and more of ferocious backlash, actively supported by the federal government, accomplished the social equivalent of putting toothpaste back in the tube. On the contrary, the right has had far more success at consolidating its political power and promoting its economic program than at reversing the cultural tide.

Cultural conservatives have made the most headway when they have focused on targets who are already unpopular or suspect, like criminal defendants, black women on welfare, teenagers who flout adult authority, "feminists" coded as man-hating and career-obsessed killjoys, professors who think there are no absolute truths, artists who get government grants for trampling on conventional morality (or worse, conventional ideas about art). When they attack divorce, day care, and unmarried mothers they may succeed in raising the national level of guilt, but ultimately they run up against Americans' uncomfortable recognition that the enemy is them—or their relatives, friends, and coworkers. (Increasingly, homosexuals are moving from the category of despised minority into that of "people we know.") For much the same reason, the right was unable to mobilize public support to remove an adulterous president.

Conservatives have stigmatized and dangerously restricted access to abortion but have not been able to arouse popular support for outlawing it. Nor has rampant hysteria about teenage sex restored the old taboos. Despite periodic censorship campaigns, open sexuality, feminist assumptions, and the iconography of multiculturalism permeate the popular media, including TV programs watched by millions; Dan Quayle's attack on *Murphy Brown* made him look sillier than his spelling. What were once radical ideas and sensibilities have been selectively assimilated not only by liberals but by a wide and politically varied swath of the population: gay Republicans demand the right to marry in the name of family values; white suburban teenagers embrace rap music and hip-hop style; evangelical Christian women roll their eyes at the Southern Baptist convention's call for wifely submission to male leadership—and in some cases their churches even leave the convention. In short, American cultural values are in flux, and Americans, pulled in conflicting directions, are ambivalent—which is why the culture wars have gone on so long and been so inconclusive.

This is not to deny that the cultural reaction has had profound effects. If it has not restored the antebellum status quo, it has nonetheless curtailed hard-won civil rights and liberties, starting with attacks on the most vulnerable groups and culminating in a jihad against the president of the United States. It has had a chilling—no, freezing—effect on any further social experiment, or even talk about it: as work, family, and morality have become bywords across the political spectrum, the implicit boundaries of "relevant" debate have virtually silenced radical social criticism in mainstream public venues. (One irony of the populist left's attacks on insular academics is that the university is the only institution of any size that still provides cultural dissidents with a platform. As a result they talk mainly to each other except when given publicity by a right indignant that they should exist at all.) Yet even as the right appeals to the electorate's sexual guilt and fear of social disorder, it has simultaneously managed to play to the other side of Americans' ambivalence: in offering dreams of wealth and power and defining as heroic rebellion the sadistic release of bashing the government, the media, the black poor and other scapegoats, conservatives have claimed the ground of freedom and pleasure that the left so readily abandoned.

In staking out all this territory, conservatives have been helped along by the cultural movements themselves. Pressure from the right long ago led many black, feminist, and gay activists to adopt a strategy of caution and appeasement, while others took refuge in moral posturing, guilt-mongering, and the celebration of group identity for its own sake. In the '80s and '90s, the ever dangerous mix of frustration and self-righteousness has propelled cultural leftists' egregious efforts to have the state and the university bureaucracies enforce their demands for political conformity, standards of sexual propriety, and attacks on free speech. Ironically, these "radical excesses" are far more in tune with the moralistic, antidemocratic temper of the conservative crackdown than with the '60s cultural radical vision, which put its faith in freedom above all. Yet both the right and anticulturalists on the left have invoked them to equate cultural radicalism with authoritarian "correctness." Since neither group has any use for the libertarians within the cultural movements, opportunism is a kind word for this maneuver, but it has played well.

Given that the culture wars have become such a one-sided affair, it's all the more remarkable that the liberatory impulse, however qualified and muted, remains a potent force in contemporary American life. What would have happened in 1994—or 1980—if desire had had a champion? Suppose—why should Charles Murray have a monopoly on "thought experiments"?—that from the '70s to the present, instead of echoing moral conservatives or changing the subject, the left had consistently argued that the point of life is to live and enjoy it fully; that genuine virtue is the overflow of happiness, not the bitter fruit of self-denial; that sexual freedom and pleasure are basic human rights; that endless work and subordination to bosses are offenses to the human spirit; that contempt for the black poor is the middle class's effort to deny that *we are next*; that mom is not going home again and so we need to rethink domestic life, child rearing, and the structures of work; that democracy is not about voting for nearly indistinguishable politicians but about having a voice in collective decision-making, not only in government, but at home, at school, at work? And suppose those arguments were coupled with a thoroughgoing critique of the new economic order and its accelerating class war, in a challenge to Americans to wrest control of their lives from the sex cops *and* the corporations?

I submit that the current political landscape would be quite different. At the very least the opposition would be on the map and able to draw some lines. The alternative is to stay in a rut so deep as to raise the bleakest of questions: is the left so afraid of freedom that it would rather lose?

Candide at Home

Watching the Dan Quayle–Murphy Brown face-off or the battles over statistics purporting to show that "illegitimacy" causes poverty and crime, you may have thought there was a real debate going on in this country about something called "family values." Actually, the debate is about who gets to win the family values pennant, a very different matter. At one time women's liberationists, radical psychoanalysts, and other cultural critics did raise serious questions about the institution of the family—about the ways it subordinates women, distorts the development of children, stifles sexuality—that were seriously discussed in public. But that was before the right-wing "pro-family" movement's successful campaign against the Equal Rights Amendment convinced mainstream feminists and social liberals that they had to "take the family issue away from the right."

Unable to endorse the conservative celebration of traditional (read patriarchal) family values, yet afraid to forthrightly oppose it, they have opted instead to redefine the issue. There is no such thing, they argue, as "the family"; there are only "families"—people living together, married or unmarried, straight or gay, in whatever arrangement they choose, so long as it is "caring" and "committed." There is no "crisis of the family," only social and economic problems that impinge on the lives of "families." Since families are just people struggling with practical problems, it follows that social welfare programs—from day care and parental leave to public housing and national health insurance—are pro-family, while the right's nostalgic fantasy of the ideal family is, on the contrary, an obstacle to helping families in the real world. Or as historian Stephanie Coontz puts it in *The Way We Never Were*, her brief for this point of view, "We must reject attempts to 'recapture' family traditions that either never existed or existed in a totally different context. Only when we have a realistic idea of how families have and have not worked in the past can we make informed decisions about how to support families in the present or improve their future prospects." It is this "progressive" version of family values—call it pro-familyism with a human face—that Murphy Brown declaimed to some twenty-four million viewers. Its assumptions, which permeate Coontz's book, have become the common sense of large sections of the urban and suburban middle class.

As her title suggests, Coontz's thesis is that the traditional family as we imagine and "remember" it is a myth, patched together out of disparate images—the cooperative extended family, the mother devoted to nurturing, the emotionally committed couple—from different historical periods. Particularly resonant are images of the so-called "Ozzie and Harriet" family of the '50s; yet this form of family, far from being traditional, was peculiarly modern, in many ways self-contradictory, and correspondingly short-lived. Overall, Coontz argues, the historical evidence shows that "families have always been in flux and often in crisis," that "there is no one family form that has ever protected people from poverty or social disruption." In the past as now, poverty affected women and children more than men (studies show, for instance, that in poor families the men were less likely to be malnourished); while there was less divorce in earlier eras, more homes were broken up by parental death, more people stayed single for their entire lives, and fewer couples described their marriages as happy. Current attempts to blame "the breakdown of the family" for the misery of the urban black poor promote stereotyped misrepresentations of black family life while ignoring unemployment, deindustrialization, the persistence of racism, and political neglect of urban problems. As

for the '5os, they were never the familial paradise they were
cracked up to be, even in white middle-class suburbia, but
were rather a period in which outward domestic cheer
masked a good deal of quiet desperation, especially among
women and girls.

I have no quarrel with this argument, as far as it goes. I find
Coontz's historical examples persuasive. I agree that familial
disruption has been taken out of context and scapegoated for
a more general social crisis. And while Coontz's analysis of
the '5os is hardly new (it informs a whole genre of '5os literature, from *The Crack in the Picture Window* to *The Lonely
Crowd,* not to mention the voluminous countercultural and
feminist writings of the '6os and '7os), in these retrograde
times it bears repeating. What bothers me about this book
and the school of thought it represents is their premise: that
the "family issue," which is arguably the central battle-
ground — and surely the central metaphor — of the bitter cultural wars of the last three decades, can be boiled down to a
conflict between misinformed nostalgia and enlightened
pragmatism. Coontz opposes myth to history, but in fact myth
too is historical. The stories we tell ourselves about the family — stories about sex and romance and morality; parental
love and protection, abuse and abandonment; children's vulnerability and rebellion — come from our psychosexual histo-
ries. They are the legacy of our childhood experience, designed as much to conceal as to reveal the bone-deep fears,
longings, and guilts that attended our passage from infancy
to adolescence within our own families. That experience, in
turn, is rooted not only in the varying circumstances of actual
families, but in the long history of the patriarchal family as an
institution: that is, the cumulative weight of laws, government, and corporate policies, religious teachings and pressures, and social norms and customs that decree what a family
is supposed to be and punish nonconformity.

In other words, for all the diversity of "families" in various times, places, and social groups, there is such a thing as "the family": a set of rules and "values," anchored in social authority and powerful, often unconscious emotions, that is far more intolerant of difference, and resistant to change, than people's actual family lives warrant. At bottom, the family issue is about whether to defend these rules in the face of massive social rebellion against them. By stigmatizing unwed childbearing and homosexuality, criminalizing abortion, making it harder to divorce, discouraging any social or economic policy that makes single motherhood easier, the right means to quell the revolt—to enforce the moral norm of lifelong monogamous marriage and punish those who flout it. "Supporting families" in their pursuit of happiness or prosperity is a secondary concern at best. From this perspective, it makes all the difference if a single-parent household is created by divorce or the choice of an unmarried woman rather than by the death of a spouse, and the dark side of the '50s family is beside the point. Indeed, the nostalgia that Coontz decries is in large part a yearning for the sense of psychic safety provided by strict norms, however onerous, as opposed to the uncertainty of freedom and the guilt stirred up by pleasure.

It is hard for pro-family progressives to see this because they themselves are ambivalent about the issues of freedom versus authority, pleasure versus sacrifice, that sustain the culture wars. Coontz's own ambivalence emerges in the second half of her book, where she turns from debunking the myth of a familial golden age to attacking the idea that feminists and working women have undermined family values and launched an epidemic of selfishness, irresponsibility, and materialism. She doesn't challenge the equation of family values with morality, or personal freedom and pleasure with selfishness. Rather, she argues that the villain is not women's rights but rampant consumerism. "Feminism," she declares, "has generally opposed consumerism; the popular association of women's equality with an individualistic, materialistic ethic occurred after the decline of organized feminism and the co-optation of 'liberated' rhetoric by the mass media and the marketing industry."

Besides being moralistic (anticonsumerism is the puritanism of the left), this analysis is simply wrong. The consumerfest unleashed by post–World War II prosperity spurred a subversive sense of entitlement to pleasure, especially among young people, that contributed directly to the cultural dissidence of the '60s, including feminism. From the beginning, the women's liberation movement took the side of the individual against familial claims. Furthermore, women's increasing ability to live outside the family, along with their demands for equality within it, have lessened men's commitment to "family values" no longer synonymous with male privilege. As I see it, Dan Quayle was right: single motherhood by choice does challenge the historic role, not to mention the historic power, of fathers. This is not just another wrinkle on "the diversity of families"; it's part of a social revolution.

Nor is anxiety about the revolt against the family merely nostalgic. A lone parent is indeed more vulnerable than two to a host of pressures; divorce does conflict with children's needs for permanence and stability. What do we tell people who are grappling with these problems — don't worry, things weren't any better in the nineteenth century? The real issue, which has been excluded from the "debate," is this: a social structure based on sexual repression and the subordination of women is breaking down, but new structures do not yet exist. The more obvious that gap becomes, the more Americans wrap themselves in the literally familiar: that communal alternatives to the family can't possibly work, and therefore need not and should not even be mentioned, is another one of those truths that "everybody knows." Yet without that discussion, there can be no honest discussion at all. And while all revolutions are scary, even for their adherents, there's no point in rejecting nostalgia only to embrace denial.

Ending Poor People As We Know Them

Early on, the opponents of welfare reform decided that their best shot was to center their argument on children. As Jason DeParle put the case in a *New York Times* article in December of 1994, "It is hard to imagine a less popular word than welfare. . . . But shift the conversation to the fate of 'poor children,' and the psychic landscape is transformed. . . . These twin forces—disdain for welfare, concern for poor children—are the seismic forces beneath the debate over public assistance. . . . It is the age-old conundrum of welfare reform: The more one seeks to punish the parent, the greater the risks to the child." DeParle saw in this contradiction an opening to the left: if child advocates could reframe the debate, Americans might be convinced that the real issue was not how to end welfare but how to end poverty.

My own observation of the psychic landscape suggested otherwise. Americans were ambivalent about much of the right's program, yet were more and more influenced by the right's cultural imagination, in which the end of welfare means the return of domestic tranquility and order, the defense of Judeo-Christian morality against a dark outlaw class that represents all the heresies of the '60s. Filtered through that vision, compassion for poor children—mixed with fear of the teenagers and adults they will become—easily slides into fatalistic pity for damned souls who should never have been born, or into fantasies of somehow rescuing the kids from their hopeless parents.

When DeParle's piece appeared, the welfare debate, like so much else, was unfolding against the backdrop of the Republican conquest of Congress. Ever since the election, the media had been promoting a right-wing myth of cultural counterrevolution that, despite its ambiguous connection to the voters' actual intentions, was fast becoming a self-fulfilling prophecy. This was not a question of partisanship. Conservatives are basically right about the press—it *is* an integral part of a cultural establishment that's essentially liberal and secular on social issues. For the most part, the mainstream media are nervous about the right, which keeps breaking their rules of civil discourse, that is, noblesse oblige and multicultural politeness. Yet as their centrist self-definition struggles with the unconscious erotic attraction of energy and power, the center drifts steadily toward the vortex.

Time, for instance, ran a cover that December depicting a scowling Gingrich, in top hat, striped pants, and goatee, as "Uncle Scrooge." " 'Tis the season to bash the poor," the cover type reads. "But is Newt Gingrich's America really that heartless?" No, the story inside argues: "In their unbridled willingness to go after immigrants and the poor, the new House firebrands may be getting out ahead of the public mood." But forget about the words; the image melds Gingrich with America as a stubborn, cranky geezer raring to, in the machoid lingo of the day, kick some ass. Just as Bruce Springsteen's "Born in the U.S.A." persona became—contrary to its protagonist's conscious intention—a Reaganite icon, Uncle Scrooge is easy to imagine on a conservative bumper sticker.

Speaking of children, *Newsweek* weighed in with a cover story on "The Orphanage: Is It Time to Bring It Back?" A box next to the headline informs us that this question refers to "The Welfare Debate," while a photographed assemblage of short-haired, poignant-looking little white kids wearing what look like white nightgowns—or are they choir robes?—hold out their hands to the viewer. What did these cherubs have to do with the welfare debate? Not much, in practical terms; a lot, symbolically speaking. As originally floated by Charles Murray and other conservatives, orphanages were simply an answer to the bleeding-heart question, "If you throw women off welfare and they can't find work, what happens to their kids?" If taking children away from their mothers seemed hard-hearted—well, ending welfare dependency was the greater good; and if these women knew their babies could be taken away, maybe they wouldn't have them in the first place. There were two problems with this formulation, however. It handed the Democrats a gold mine of righteous rhetoric about Dickens, and it seemed to contradict family values. So a new rationale began to surface: kids are better off in orphanages than in the chaotic, lawless culture of the underclass, with no fathers and abusive, neglectful, drug-addicted mothers incapable of giving them a moral foundation. *Newsweek*'s piece is dutifully balanced—on the one hand Oliver Twist, on the other, "the concern, now verging on panic, for the catastrophic decline of proper child-rearing practices among the poor." But its imagery—like Gingrich's bizarre, Reaganesque suggestion that Hillary Clinton watch *Boys Town*—promotes the subliminal fantasy that welfare reform can save civilization by transforming all those fearsome, unsocialized black kids into Mickey Rooney. In short, it's the deep, unconscious appeal of the right's worldview that drives the framing of political issues, not the other way around.

I should say that I don't think orphanages, group homes, or whatever we want to call them, are inherently a bad idea for children whose parents are absent, abusive, or neglectful—as opposed to merely poor—and who are unlikely to be adopted. By giving kids the security of a place they can count on, long-term placement in a group home could be a lot better than foster care, with its assumption of impermanence — an assumption so basic to its definition that kids have actually been taken away from foster parents judged to be "too attached." Of course, to even begin to meet children's emotional needs, group homes would have to be small, with enough staff to give the kids (especially infants and toddlers) individual attention, and surrogate parents who saw their jobs as a long-term professional commitment. Though such homes do exist, making them widely available would cost a fortune. Since welfare reformers have no intention of spending that kind of money, any discussion of orphanages that pretends it's about helping kids, rather than demonizing parents, is frivolous and hypocritical.

But then, the same could be said of the whole sorry discussion about welfare, which as it turns out was never a debate in any meaningful sense, only an argument among undertakers about how to dispose of the body. At bottom, the logic of the attack on welfare mothers is that the poor should stop breeding altogether and solve the problem of the underclass by disappearing. "To bring a child into the world," the ubiquitous Murray declared in *Commentary*, "knowing that you are not intellectually, emotionally, or materially ready to care for that child is *wrong*." Leaving aside that obnoxious "intellectually" — the man is obsessed with poor people's IQs — who in good conscience can disagree? But consider the context. Murray is not only talking about teenage mothers here; he means that parents should have jobs and be married. Especially married: "Illegitimacy is the central social problem of our time." The most crucial purpose of welfare reform is to "generate a situation in which a young woman is . . . so scared at the prospect of getting pregnant that she will not have intercourse, or will take care not to get pregnant if she does." Having a child out of wedlock should be, as it once was, "so immediately, tangibly punishing that it overrides everything else. . . . Subtle moral reasoning is not the response that works. 'My father would kill me' is the kind of response that works."

With this tirade, Murray has crossed the boundaries of welfare polemic into the classless terrain of patriarchal terrorism. Yet for the poor women who are its immediate targets, it poses another layer of problems. Fear of unwed motherhood might give them an "incentive" to marry, but without any chance for the privilege and status that come with breadwinning, why would poor, unemployed men go along? Nor do the poorest women have much prospect of *ever* earning enough money to support children adequately. Nor, of course, do Murray's politics allow for any kind of collective social commitment to alleviating the debilitating poverty and social demoralization that affect people's ability to care for their children. There is in fact no way for most indigent women to be "ready" for motherhood in Murray's terms. Nonetheless, most people, whatever their class, have a powerful desire to reproduce, and communities are unlikely to assent to their own annihilation on moral grounds. What happens when we cut the poor off welfare and they still won't go away?

What We Don't Talk about When We Talk about The Bell Curve

Around the same time that an insurgent right-wing Congress was taking charge of American politics, a parallel cultural event occurred: the publication of Charles Murray and the late Richard Herrnstein's *The Bell Curve*. This massive work was really two books. One was a media event designed to fill a conspicuous gap in public discourse—while the figures on crime and "illegitimacy" had long served to release sensitive white people from their pesky inhibitions about calling blacks violent and hypersexual, in recent years there had been no comparable statistical outlet for the sentiment that blacks are dumb. The other, which lurked obscurely in the shadow of the public conversation, was a polemic about the intelligentsia or, as the authors called it, the "cognitive elite." The first book presented IQ as the preeminent criterion of social worth; the second attacked intelligence as a means of allocating social power. Contradictory as they sounded, these arguments nonetheless converged in a paradoxical vision: invoking the authority of science, *The Bell Curve* rejected the whole enterprise of modernity.

Conservatives are perennially tempted by the illusion that vexing social conflicts can be settled by exposing radical aspirations to the dry air of "the facts." Twenty-five years ago, Steven Goldberg thought he could prove "the inevitability of patriarchy" by citing studies that linked aggression with testosterone and concluded that men were innately more aggressive than women. (As far as I can tell, this line of argument has had no effect on sexual politics except to inspire mock diagnoses of "testosterone poisoning.") Fifteen years ago, right-to-life activists imagined that the expansion of scientific knowledge about fetal development would have to change people's minds about abortion. Now *The Bell Curve*'s revival of decades-old claims about IQ — that there is such a thing as a quantifiable general intelligence; that IQ tests measure it accurately and objectively; that it is largely genetic, highly resistant to change, and unevenly distributed among races; that high IQ correlates with economic and social success, low IQ with the abject condition and aberrant behavior of the poor — is supposed to tell us what to do about social equality, namely, abandon the idea as quixotic. Yet to argue about the meaning of IQ — as about the humanity of fetuses or the nature of sexual difference — is really a way of defusing anxiety by displacing onto impersonal "factual" dispute a profound clash of interests and worldviews, with all the yearning, hatred, and fear that clash entails. If I bought the authors' thesis, I would still be allergic to their politics. I don't advocate equality because I think everyone is the same; I believe that difference, real or imagined, is no excuse for subordinating some people to others. Equality is a principle of human relations, not Procrustes' bed.

In fact, the authors tacitly recognize that science is not the key issue here. Recounting the history of the IQ debate, they focus less on the substance of the argument than on the struggle to prevail as the conventional wisdom. As they tell it, their view of intelligence and IQ testing was taken for granted until it ran into the dogmatic egalitarianism of the '60s and '70s, when Herrnstein, Arthur Jensen, and others who correlated race and class differences with IQ scores were driven out of the public arena by intimidating demonstrations and intellectual antagonists like Stephen Jay Gould; but although the latter "won the visible battle," discussion of the significance of IQ continued to take place offstage. The clear implication of this tale of exile is that with the rightward shift in the nation's politics, it's time for the return.

In short, *The Bell Curve* is not about breaking new intellectual ground, but about coming up from underground. Murray and Herrnstein are convinced "that the topic of genes, intelligence, and race in the late twentieth century is like the topic of sex in Victorian England. Publicly, there seems to be nothing to talk about. Privately, people are fascinated by it." I can't quarrel with this point. The idea that black brains are genetically inferior to white brains did not fade from public view simply because white people were convinced by Stephen Jay Gould's eloquent arguments. Rather, the gap between Americans' conscious moral consensus for racial equality and the tenacious social and psychic structures of racism was papered over with guilt and taboo. Many opponents of racism thought they were doing their political duty by shouting down the Jensens and Herrnsteins, driving them underground. But this literal enforcement of taboo was only a crude reflection of a much more widespread process of self-censorship.

I don't mean that the moral consensus of the post–civil rights era wasn't genuine. I mean that morality isn't enough, that it can't forever keep the lid on contrary feelings rooted in real social relationships that have not been understood, confronted, or transformed. Commenting on *The Bell Curve* in the *New Republic,* John B. Judis indignantly points out that the taboo Murray and Herrnstein are so proud of violating was a reaction to Nazism: "It's not a taboo against unflinching scientific inquiry, but against pseudo-scientific racism. Of all the world's taboos, it is most deserving of retention." The problem, though, is that taboos can never truly vanquish the powerful desires that provoke them. For some decades after the Holocaust, there was a moratorium on open anti-Semitism in Europe and America; it didn't last. So long as hierarchy is a ruling principle of our culture, a basic fact of everyday life, the idea of black inferiority cannot be transcended, only repressed. And in an era when an ascendant global capitalism is creating a new, worldwide class structure—when the language of social Darwinism is increasingly regarded as a simple description of reality—genetic determination of social status is an idea whose time has come back.

The media blitz began with Murray's picture on the cover of the *New York Times Magazine,* its headline a classic self-fulfilling prophecy: "The Most Dangerous Conservative." "Over a decade," the cover type continued, "Charles Murray has gained ground in his crusade to abolish welfare. But now, with his contentious views on I.Q., class and race, has he gone too far?" The accompanying profile was critical of Murray's views. But the real message of the article lay in its existence, its prominence, and the assumption embedded in its presentation—that *The Bell Curve* had pushed the American public debate to a new and daring frontier, with all the disreputable glamour such an undertaking implied (and incidentally had outflanked Murray's crusade to abolish welfare, which was now respectable—hadn't Clinton all but endorsed it?).

Subsequent coverage continued in this vein, proclaiming through sheer volume and visibility that *The Bell Curve* was a serious work whose thesis, however unpalatable, could not be ignored. *Newsweek*'s cover featured a Janus-like white face and black face turned away from each other (was it my imagination, or did the black face look a little like O. J. Simpson?) on either side of the headline, "IQ: Is It Destiny?" The front page of the *New York Times Book Review*—which reviewed *The Bell Curve* and a number of other books making biological-determinist arguments in the same issue—asked, "How Much Of Us Is in the Genes?" (Note the ubiquitous question as ass-covering device. Is it destiny? Hey, we're not saying it is, we're not saying it isn't.) The *New Republic*'s cover, in huge type, simply read "Race & I. Q."; virtually the entire issue was devoted to an article by Murray and Herrnstein, based on material from the book, and nineteen (!) replies. Murray's TV appearances and countless op-eds hammered the theme home: attention must be paid.

Most of this commentary was hostile. Some of it noted that *The Bell Curve*'s thesis was not new but a rehash of ideas with a long and dubious pedigree. It would not have been an implausible reaction if editors had rolled their eyes at Murray's getting in bed with the IQ crowd, if they'd felt the kind of embarrassment one feels when, say, a respected intellectual joins a religious cult. Instead, it seemed that their dominant emotion was fear of being or being called a censor. I can't help suspecting that that fear had less to do with a healthy respect for debate than with the cultural unconscious of a white, educated middle class projecting onto an Evil But Courageous book its own tabooed racial feelings.

Not coincidentally, the media's treatment of *The Bell Curve* centered obsessively on race and virtually ignored class, which is the book's main subject (its subtitle is *Intelligence and Class Structure in American Life*). Murray and Herrnstein clearly invited this reaction, not only by including a section on race and repackaging it for the *New Republic,* but by devoting so much space to their dire view of the underclass—while they warn of an "emerging white underclass," elsewhere in the book, as in the public conversation generally, the word is code for "black." Still, it seems peculiar that journalists, certified members of *The Bell Curve*'s "cognitive elite," should have so little comment on its analysis of their own class status. Their silence is one more piece of evidence that even as economic restructuring makes class an issue in more and more people's lives, they stubbornly resist talking about it. It strikes me, in fact, that blackness has become as much a code for "underclass" as the other way around—that when whites treat middle-class black men in suits and ties like potential muggers and rapists, what they fear is being engulfed and tainted by lower-classness. It's a truism that poor whites embrace racism so they can see the lower class as safely Other. But in the new, anarchic world order, the specter of downward mobility haunts us all.

The Bell Curve's class analysis goes like this: At an earlier time, when social classes were sorted out by birth and there were many fewer specialized occupations that demand high intelligence, cognitive ability was distributed fairly evenly throughout the class structure. Now equal opportunity— particularly equal access to higher education—and the shift toward a high-tech, knowledge-based economy have made intelligence the main agent of class stratification. (If you're tempted to tune out right here—equal opportunity? what are they talking about?—bear with me. The argument gets more interesting.) As the brainy rise to the top and the dull-witted sink to the increasingly miserable bottom, social proximity makes people ever more likely to mate within their own cognitive group (a tendency exacerbated by feminism, which encourages educated men in high IQ jobs to marry similarly situated women). That accelerates the process of IQ stratification, since (to quote one of the summaries for the cognitively impaired that precede each chapter) "as America equalizes the circumstances of people's lives, the remaining differences in intelligence are increasingly determined by differences in genes."

As a result, the authors worry, the cognitive elite is coalescing "into a class of its own." Smart people are socialized in similar ways and isolated from the TV/tabloid/talk radio culture of ordinary Americans. They have exploited the increasing reach of the federal government since the '6os to impose their values on the rest of society. And now, as the rich get brighter and the bright get richer, a scary confluence looms: "Do you think," Murray and Herrnstein ask rhetorically, "that the rich in America already have too much power? Or do you think the intellectuals already have too much power? . . . just watch what happens as their outlooks and interests converge." A probable consequence, in the authors' view, is that a large class of smart, affluent people (10 to 20 percent of the population) will wall itself off from the rest of society, particularly from the threatening underclass, withdrawing from public institutions and preferring to pay for its own private services. Still clinging to its belief in the welfare state, even as it loses faith that the poor can improve their condition, this class will most likely use its power to institute "the custodial state"—"an expanded welfare state for the underclass that also keeps it out from underfoot."

How to avoid this dystopia? What people need, *The Bell Curve* argues, is a "valued place" in the social order. In traditional societies, people across the cognitive spectrum attained this "valued place" through work, community, and family. As occupations that don't require a high IQ lose prestige and earning power, it is harder and harder for the dull to find a valued place at work. This makes community and family all the more important, yet these sources of valued place have also been undercut. And much of the blame for this situation rests on, you guessed it, the CE's misguided attitudes and values. For one thing, "the federal domination of public policy that has augmented the cognitive elite's political leverage during the last 3o years . . . has had the collateral effect of stripping the neighborhood of much of the stuff of life." This hasn't bothered the CE because its members aren't centered in a geographic community but are oriented to the nation and the world. Furthermore, the CE is now running American society by rules that people with low or even ordinary IQs find too difficult to follow. These rules are based on the idea that "complicated, sophisticated operationalizations of fairness, justice, and right and wrong are ethically superior to simple, black-and-white versions." Such rules "give the cognitive elite the greatest advantage," since "deciphering complexity is one of the things that cognitive ability is most directly good for."

In the crucial area of morality, for instance, society should make it easy for dullards to be virtuous by making simple rules about crime and punishment that everyone enthusiastically enforces. But the CE with its complicated rules and moral ambiguities has produced a confusing system where the bad guys don't always lose, and worse, people don't always agree on what's bad. Similarly, the CE's sexual revolution has made it more difficult for the dull "to figure out why marriage is a good thing, and, once in a marriage . . . to figure out why

45

one should stick with it through bad times." Marriage is satisfying to the extent that society unequivocally upholds it as an institution; the CE supports the right to sex and procreation outside marriage and demands legal and social recognition of nonmarital relationships.

This broadside against the *clercs* has enough contradictions to keep the critics busy (for one thing, the increasing reliance of the affluent on private rather than public services, which the authors view with alarm, is a direct result of the governmental shrinkage they champion). But a more serious problem is the fanciful nature of its central conceit—the supposed ruling coalition of the rich and the smart, which lumps together the titans of the global marketplace and people like me. Since I belong to the CE if anyone does (skipped a grade in junior high school, graduated from a Seven Sisters college, work in not one but two knowledge industries, managed to get through 845 pages of *The Bell Curve* with a minimum of cheating), how come I'm not running the World Bank?

In the real world, intellectuals and techies not directly tied into the production of wealth are fast following blue-collar workers into redundancy. Technology eliminates intellectual along with manual labor; white-collar jobs migrate to countries whose newly educated classes are willing to work at lower rates; obsession with the bottom line translates into suspicion of any intellectual work whose productivity can't be easily measured. Companies are shedding managers and replacing engineers and computer programmers with machines. The job markets in the academy and the publishing industry are dismal, support for artists and writers even scarcer than usual, the public and nonprofit sectors—hotbeds of cognitive elitism—steadily shrinking. Nor are card-carrying CE members exempt from the pervasive trend toward employment of part-time, temporary, and benefit-free workers. Wealth is increasingly concentrated at the top and, last I looked, still handily outstrips other sources of power.

Still, I do have something in common with the Walter Wristons, the Rupert Murdochs, the venture capitalists in Eastern Europe—that deeply suspect tropism for locating the center of our lives outside the neighborhood. Like genetic theories of racial inferiority, antipathy toward intellectuals and capitalists on the grounds of their rootless cosmopolitanism is a recurring theme among reactionaries whose loyalties are more aristocratic than bourgeois. And for all the authors' lip service to the American ideals of meritocracy and equal opportunity (as opposed to equal results), their vision of the good society is essentially feudal: it's that old chestnut the organic community, where there is "A Place for Everyone" (a chapter heading) and all cheerfully accept their place, while a kindly but firm, paternal ruling class runs things according to rules even the darkies can understand. Equality of opportunity unleashes the disruptive force of intelligence, deposes the organic hierarchy, and rends the social fabric. In effect, *The Bell Curve* restates a core belief of unreconstructed conservatives (not the free-market kind): that the Enlightenment ruined culture.

Yet Murray and Herrnstein, themselves part of the elite they decry, are nothing if not free-marketeers; despite their suggestion that the rich are too powerful, their targets are government and culture, not the economic system. On the surface, this doesn't make sense: do they seriously imagine that capitalism can somehow be divorced from its cosmopolitan character, and that if only the government and the CE would get out of the way, community and family would provide the underclass with a valued place? But a deeper logic is at work here. Murray and Herrnstein don't really object to the power of wealth; they're merely willing to appeal to resent-

ment of the rich to bolster their argument against intellectuals and their subversive ways. Who, after all, is the *you* they're
addressing with those rhetorical questions? Clearly, "the average American," whom the authors regard as "an asset, not
part of the problem," and who, they imply, would do fine were
it not for the oppressive power of the cognitive elite and the
burdensome underclass its policies have nurtured. By this
route, *The Bell Curve*'s aristocratic outlook merges seamlessly
with right-wing populism.

The Bell Curve, with its dry academic tone and pages of statistics, is not in itself a powerful book. But it rides a powerful
wave of emotion—the frustration of a middle class that, whatever its IQ scores, sees its choices narrowing, its future in
doubt. Rejecting the moral taboos of the left to flirt with the
shameless brutality of the right feels like a hit of freedom. But
like all drugs it wears off, leaving the underlying problem untouched. The danger is that Americans will seek out more and
bigger doses, while radicalism remains the greatest taboo of
all.

Rodney King's Revenge

Call me the last innocent in America, but the day the O. J.
Simpson verdict came in, I thought a conviction was possible,
even likely. Paradoxically, it was Detective Mark Fuhrman's lurid tape-recorded spew that made me think so. Here was this
guy, the personification or nightmare caricature of the law
gone rotten, the cop as racist vigilante (with a name from
the same root as "führer," no less), and yet his exposure had
failed—or so it seemed to me—to make a serious dent in the
prosecution's case. Simpson's history of violence against Nicole was damning, even without the evidence Judge Ito had
disallowed. There was simply too much physical evidence to
be entirely invalidated by the bungling that had surrounded

its collection; and deliberately falsifying that evidence would have required an elaborate conspiracy that required too much coordination and disciplined silence, among too many people with no discernible motive, to be remotely plausible. In any case, it didn't make sense that policemen who had protected Simpson in the past, and hesitated to arrest him for the murders, would want to frame him. And in the absence of such a plot, the Fuhrman tape, however shocking, was irrelevant.

Most juries, when it comes down to the wire, take their job seriously; surely, I thought, in a world-is-watching case like this, the jurors' pride in their role, their sense of the gravity and public import of their decision, will prevail. Wasn't it, in a genteel middle-class way, as racist as Fuhrman's rantings to assume that black jurors would act reflexively to free a black celebrity or stick it to the LAPD? And when the decision came back so quickly, I knew it had to be "guilty." True, quick verdicts were usually acquittals, but in this case it was inconceivable that twelve people could let their man off without a long and bloody argument. So I began mentally composing my *Village Voice* column, along the lines of how whites had been carried away by racial paranoia and blacks by dreams of Rodney King's revenge, but in the end the jury had chosen reality over fantasy and history over myth.

In the column I actually wrote, I told this story. In response I got an angry letter from a black woman who accused me of wanting the Simpson jurors to "rise above race" to reassure me that I had nothing to worry about. I was embarrassed to realize she was right. That moment of recognition didn't change my opinion of the verdict, but it made clear that wherever one stood in relation to this Rorschach test of the century, there was little enough innocence to go around. Not that I had ever imagined my view of O. J. Simpson was unconditioned by my overall view of the world. In truth, the moment I

49

knew he had beaten Nicole, I found him guilty. To me it was clear that the same mania for control that had led him to beat her had ultimately led him to kill her. I also thought he deserved to be put away whether he had actually committed murder or not. While various commentators, in the days after his arrest, suggested that people felt they knew O. J. and therefore wouldn't want to see him executed, I found Simpson's history of unpunished brutality so infuriating that I lusted to kill him myself (which I guess means I could hold my own in a presidential debate) and include a few cops, judges, and freeway cheerleaders for good measure. Of course, had I been on the jury, I would have made every effort to put my preconceptions aside and weigh the evidence; I believe in the principle of a fair trial. But that's what they all say (and what, in fact, the jurors said). The point is, I knew my story had a gendered spin. I shouldn't have been surprised that it had a racial spin as well.

In view of the acquittal and its aftermath, it's easy to forget that racial fantasy was inseparable from the Simpson case long before Johnnie Cochran started spinning it—as early as the controversial *Time* cover with the "photo illustration" of O. J. that darkened his skin a few shades. The "American Tragedy" *Time* proclaimed on that cover referred less to Simpson's downfall, in itself, than to white Americans' continually thwarted quest for a painless solution to their Negro problem. O. J. the good, the friendly, the easygoing, the generous, the black man who transcended race, who "had it all"—have you ever heard that obnoxious concept applied to anyone not black and/or female?—was a deeply soothing figure. Simpson with a "dark" side was anything but. Indeed, he became fodder for a particularly insidious form of white paranoia: no matter how much one of "them" appears to be one of us, underneath they are all rampaging brutes. The *New York Post* blurted it best, in a front-page headline: "O. J. and Coke:

Drugs Fueled His Rage." Or so "friends and acquaintances of Nicole" reportedly told columnist Andrea Peyser. An accompanying story cited "police sources in Buffalo" as claiming that "Simpson narrowly missed being nailed in two major drug raids in 1975." Note how this formulation transmutes the iconography from "man abusing woman" to "another crazed black guy on drugs."

Just as Simpson's beating of Nicole Brown, though a matter of public record, had had no impact on his pristine image; just as the media indulged in weeks of maudlin Othello analogies before picking up on the domestic violence theme; so O. J.'s defense shifted the focus of his trial from violence against women and the way men get away with it to a classic black-man-versus-racist-police scenario. In the process, Nicole was demoted from a central character in the drama to its mere occasion. And as race became its main theme, while gender disappeared, a familiar lacuna was revealed: "race" referred entirely to the situation of black men in relation to white authority. Black women, who have no little experience of domestic violence, didn't count. In that respect, the trajectory of the Simpson trial recalled the Clarence Thomas hearings, where Thomas appropriated blackness with his "high tech lynching" rhetoric, while Anita Hill was deracialized, defined by the media, Thomas's allies, and many black people as a surrogate white feminist.

The Rodney King case was the wrong grid to lay on O. J. Simpson. It didn't fit the crime, it diverted the jury from what should have been its job, and it led to a miscarriage of justice. But it's a misreading to equate the verdict, as some commentators did, with the South's old habit of routinely acquitting whites who committed crimes against blacks. The message of those acquittals was that whites had the right to kill blacks to keep them in their place. This jury did not act out of animus toward the victims because of their race, or Nicole because of her sex; it didn't imply that their deaths were a good thing for the social order; it simply ignored them, which was bad enough.

The southern comparison was the most overwrought position in a generally reductive debate. One side accused the jurors of nullification, pure and simple—of ignoring the evidence and freeing Simpson out of racial solidarity and/or to "send a message" to the LAPD. The other insisted that they had weighed the evidence, including the credibility of police witnesses, and had reasonable doubts—and furthermore, anyone who imagined otherwise was guilty of stereotyping blacks, especially black women, as "emotional" and "irrational." The problem with both arguments is their common assumption that evidence speaks for itself, or should. In reality, the way any jury perceives a body of evidence depends heavily on the stories the lawyers weave around it. And the Simpson defense wove a compelling story of police incompetence, mendacity, and racism. Told to a mostly black jury inclined to admire O. J. and believe the worst of LA cops, that story had the power to reduce the prosecution's mountain of evidence to a pile of tainted rubble. At the same time, in putting Fuhrman on trial and casting Simpson as his victim, it overshadowed the People's narrative: the story of genial O. J. as Mr. Hyde, stalking, battering, and finally butchering the ex-wife he couldn't control.

Yet the card Cochran played had arguably been dealt by his opponents. Simpson was hardly a natural for the role of oppressed black man, given his wealth, celebrity, and raceless persona; the LA police, far from harassing him, had been all too indulgent of his "domestic disputes." It would seem to be the D. A. who reinvented him in the mold of Rodney King, letting the fear that Simpson would be convicted by an all-white jury and touch off another riot dictate the downtown venue of the trial (though Marcia Clark insists that any case of such major proportions would have had to be tried there). The prosecution then conveniently delivered the racist cop, out of a baffling hubris—or perhaps a profound unconscious urge to replay the King movie with a different ending. Clark also admits, in her autobiography, that she saw her cause as basically doomed from the moment she confronted a jury pool she deemed so hopeless that she didn't bother to use all her peremptory challenges. I don't doubt that her chances of prevailing were slim; yet her attitude toward the jury blurs the line between rational pessimism and a defeatism that may have amounted to self-fulfilling prophecy. A lawyer blaming defeat on a closed-minded jury—especially before the fact— is a bit like a psychotherapist complaining that the patient doesn't want to get well: the charge may be true, but it's not terribly useful. Penetrating the psyche of a hostile jury, finding ways to make the elusive connection, is basic to a trial lawyer's skill. It follows that failure to connect reflects the lawyer's limitations as well as the jurors'.

Could the prosecution have done more to disrupt the defense's story and foreground its own? Clark and Christopher Darden knew almost from the start that Fuhrman was a dicey character. They didn't believe his professed innocence of racial slurs; Darden even wanted to declare him a hostile witness. Shouldn't they have investigated, found witnesses who would discredit him, and expressed preemptive shock and horror, rather than merely putting him on the stand and hoping nothing damaging would come out? Clark is impatient with such questions. As far as she's concerned, Cochran should not have brought race into his defense, and Ito should not have allowed it—enough said. But in the trial of a black male celebrity accused of murdering two white people, against the backdrop of post–Rodney King Los Angeles, race was going to be present in the courtroom; the only question was how openly or covertly.

As for the domestic violence story, Clark acknowledges that although "deep down I knew [it] lay at the center of the case," she pursued it halfheartedly. She was leery of being thought to "spout a feminist line" or condone "the culture of victimization." She recognized in herself an "emotional resistance" to the issue, apparently related to memories of being raped as a teenager and having shoving matches with her possessive first husband. And she doubted the jury would buy it—a sentiment that clearly reflected her own ambivalence as well as her corroding doubt that the jury would buy anything.

Among whites outraged by the verdict, and by the popular support it enjoyed in the black community, there was much apocalyptic talk about the damage it had supposedly done to race relations (in one of her more hyperbolic moments, Clark in effect blames Johnnie Cochran for the passage of California's anti–affirmative action proposition). Those who, like me, were more anguished than outraged were inclined to dwell on what seemed to be the separate and incommensurable realities that stared at each other from across the racial divide. In my column, I suggested that what we were seeing was something even more alarming: the breakdown of belief in any possibility of a good-faith struggle toward some consensual version of truth, a breakdown that did not start with black jurors but with mostly white intellectuals—talk about chickens coming home to roost! In retrospect, this observation, while not entirely false, strikes me as melodramatic. That even eyewitnesses tend to give wildly divergent accounts of the same event; that this endemically human problem is aggravated by social conflict; that some see it not as a problem but as an affirmation of difference—all this complicates our every endeavor from justice to politics to love. The Simpson trial is not the first nor will it be the last proof of that truism, though it may well be the best publicized.

My father, a retired New York City policeman, has his own

take on the infamous Fuhrman tape: he thinks it was a put-on, a typical example of the way cops love to scandalize civilians with exaggerated accounts of their own badness. I like this idea; it appeals to my sense of irony as well as explaining why Fuhrman would confide in a stranger about conduct that was not only reprehensible but illegal. It doesn't absolve Fuhrman, whose racism and sexism are well-documented from other sources; anyway, the purpose of such bad-cop tales, true or not, is to intimidate (as my father sees it, the more terrifying civilians' idea of what cops are capable of, the better for the crime rate). But it adds a new wrinkle to the question of those ever shifting, permeable boundaries between fantasy and fact that make up the stuff of how we live now. When I relayed my father's theory to my black male editor, he had his own story to tell: a cop had stopped him on the highway, supposedly for speeding but really for having a white female passenger. On the side of the road was a steel barrier. The cop kept ordering Joe to pull up closer and closer to the barrier, till finally he had no choice but to scratch his car. Fuhrman may have been fantasizing, but one person's fantasy can be another person's fact.

Marcia Clark should have kept that in mind. One of the more poignant passages of her memoir reveals that in the end she convinced herself that physical evidence was all she really needed. "Blood would tell the truth," she thought. How ironic that a woman who believed in the importance of her own story, urgently enough to write a book, should forget an elementary fact: blood doesn't talk — people do.

Million Man Mirage

For the obvious antiseparatist, antisexist, anti–family values, anti–moral uplift, anti-bootstrap, anticapitalist, antifascist, and anti–O. J. Simpson reasons, I hated the whole idea of the Million Man March. But as celebratory reviews from marchers and onlookers—some of whom had been skeptical or even hostile beforehand—kept coming in, I had to conclude that either a sizable portion of the black community had been taken over by pod people, or something significant had happened that wasn't covered by my social and political categories.

What I kept hearing about was peace, love, connection, freedom from tension and suspicion. While the press insisted on making comparisons to the 1963 Martin Luther King march, the analogy that sprang irresistibly if somewhat queasily to my mind was Woodstock. On that occasion, half a million people had seized the opportunity to convert what looked like sure disaster into a spectacular exercise of collective will to live out a utopian moment. Amid the ecstatic accounts of the participants, sympathetically passed along by the media, it was considered impolite if not downright mean to mention certain other aspects of the festival—like the incompetence and dangerous irresponsibility of its promoters, or the enormous amount of work and taxpayers' money involved in making emergency provisions for food, water, and sanitation, or even the terrible weather. On the other hand, to have focused on such complaints and ignored the utopian moment would have been to miss the story.

I don't want to push this analogy too far. Woodstock was the invention of affluent white kids with an expansive sense of entitlement, self-proclaimed countercultural missionaries to America. The marchers were mainly middle-class black guys, coming together not to declare a cultural revolution but to contest their demonization as culturally alien, inferior, and criminal. The point, though, is that utopian moments are basically alike: there's the falling away of the convoluted layers of embattlement and mutual paranoia that stand in the way of simple human contact; the melting of the psychic fortress; the freedom from a loneliness more terrible than you knew; the knowledge that it's okay, really okay, to relax. At such a moment Louis Farrakhan, anti-Semitism, the carapace of masculinism would be irrelevant—concerns from another dimension.

But utopian moments have something else in common—transience. Insofar as they challenge cynicism and encourage the faith that it's possible to live differently, to be different, they do change people, but not in any predictable direction: the myriad utopian moments shared by psychedelic trippers in the '60s produced born-again Christians and Buddhist stockbrokers as well as anarchists. Only movements with particular social visions and practical goals can give faith a concrete, real-world shape, which is to say it's a mistake to imagine that the good feelings generated by the Million Man March negate its awful politics.

Yet this is exactly what a lot of black and white liberals have claimed. Before the march, its defenders argued for distinguishing the message from the messenger. When feminists pointed out that part of the message was that women should stay home and men should resume their rightful place as head of the family, a subtle rhetorical shift occurred: now skeptics were urged to endorse not the "message" but the "purpose" of the march. What was that purpose, exactly? Vague inspirational generalities ensued, along with a perceptible irritation. After the march, its emotional power became the focus of the discussion, inspiring paeans to brotherhood and unity and, on the flip side, what I think of as the Let-a-Hundred-Flowers-Bloom theory of the event. WNYC's *On the Line* aired a conversation between black sociologist Joyce Ladner and me, in which she laid out this perspective: Farrakhan and the Nation of Islam and their ideology have nothing to do with why the marchers were there or what the march meant to them; each man's view of the march reflected his own unique reality, and each would respond to this energizing experience in his own way, whether that meant starting freedom schools or registering people to vote.

Ladner also said that as "a womanist and a feminist," she had no problem with the men-only march. As she saw it, this wasn't about patriarchy but about men getting their act together so they could give black women some help. Some younger black women I talked to said they disagreed with the patriarchal paternalism stuff and couldn't take it seriously; black women weren't about to stay home and submit. Still, they supported the march. Black men, they argued, are so disconnected and demoralized, the first priority is to get them to come back and get involved with women, with their kids — then we'll worry about equality.

All mass mobilizations have a life of their own. Almost by definition, they appeal to broad discontents rather than narrow ideological agendas; most people aren't ideologues. But this hardly means that who leads them, and what those leaders are saying, doesn't matter. The dismissal of Farrakhan's importance reminds me of the confidence with which Iranian and American leftists argued, during Khomeini's revolution, that the people were in the streets to oppose the shah, not to support a religious fanatic. If Farrakhan was so incidental to the whole affair, how come it was Farrakhan and not someone else who pulled it off?

The answer, it seems to me, has everything to do with the bankruptcy of liberalism and the vacuum that gapes where a radical left should be. Faced with a deepening racial crisis and the right's relentless class war, "progressives" haven't the least idea what to do beyond clinging to the shards of the New Deal. On the cultural front, the superiority of the two-parent family has become such an unquestioned assumption that it's taboo to acknowledge the obvious: among whites as well as blacks, the institution of marriage is in trouble because its underpinning is women's subordination. The disengagement that black women — and more and more white women — complain of reflects men's resentment at being deprived of dominance in the family, whether because they're too poor to support a household or because of women's increasing economic independence and insistence on equality. And though most women want men to share their lives and parental responsibilities, they're not willing to put up with the old terms. Exhorting men to do the right thing is not going to resolve these conflicts; what we need is to reinvent the family for a post-patriarchal world. But anyone who says so is accused of spouting hippy-dippy nonsense.

In the circumstances, it's hardly surprising that black men flocked to a Farrakhan march, or that black women supported it, any more than it's surprising that whites voted for the Gingrich Congress. Most blacks don't subscribe to Farrakhan's more extreme views, but then most whites don't subscribe to the Republican right's more extreme views. It's just that there's no serious competition out there. Who among the assorted black politicians and civil rights establishmentarians currently passing for leaders is capable of organizing a militant mass movement or even aspires to do such a thing? Even Jesse Jackson, the left's great black hope, could never quite decide who he was. He wanted to be progressive without alienating the nationalists, nationalist without alienating the Jews, socially conservative *and* feminist. One minute he's arguing for a rainbow coalition, the next he's back on Farrakhan's platform. Who can trust the guy? Nor did he ever get serious about building a movement. Farrakhan, in contrast, knows exactly who he is: a skilled organizer with a vision and a program. He isn't afraid of offending white people or Jews; on the contrary, he revels in giving offense. With his own powerful persona, he conveys the hope of power to black men,

indeed to many black women as well. To imagine that his
appeal is confined to people who subscribe to the Nation of
Islam's tenets is to deny history's lessons about the unconscious and the way charisma works.

In any case, the political impact of the march was not confined to the marchers themselves. White America respects
success, and the media were clearly impressed with Farrakhan's achievement. He is a player now in a way he wasn't before, no longer a marginal antiwhite extremist but the leader
of a massive peaceful demonstration in favor of work, family,
self-help—in essence, the Republican program. Sure, he's
anti-Semitic, but as many observers have noted, this never
kept Pat Buchanan or Pat Robertson out of the mainstream.

The most potent message the march transmitted was that
blacks are now ready to be part of the pro-family solution instead of the problem. Though its moralism was for once
aimed at men, it inevitably reinforces the right's attacks on
single mothers and "illegitimacy." Predictably, the *Wall Street
Journal,* in a post-march editorial, crowed that the event
showed Dan Quayle was right. When I brought this up on the
radio, Joyce Ladner scoffed that most of the people who
marched don't read the *Wall Street Journal* and aren't affected
by it. This is silly: we're all affected by one of the most influential newspapers in the country whether we read it or not. But
don't take it from the *WSJ,* take it from the president of the
National Urban League, who told *Time,* "I think this may have
been the largest family-values rally in the history of America."
I listened for a hint of irony, but heard none.

Villains and Victims

When Marx amended Hegel to specify that history repeats itself, the first time as tragedy, the second as farce, he could

have been talking about the history of American sexual politics from Anita Hill to Paula Jones and Monica Lewinsky. From the beginning conservatives used Jones's case not only to attack Bill Clinton but to accuse feminists of a hypocritical double standard. "Paula Stunned by Feminists' Silence," a headline in the right-wing *New York Post* observed, while in the *New York Times* Maureen Dowd offered such tidbits as that redoubtable neanderthal, Representative Bob Dornan, suddenly converted to the cause of fighting sexual harassment, sporting an "I believe Paula" button. While these complaints, however disingenuous, pointed to an uncomfortable truth—most publicly visible feminists had reacted to Jones's charges with reflexive avoidance, and some with inexcusable class snobbery—they had little impact, since Paula was perceived by most people to the left of Dornan as a tool of the sectarian right. But with the breaking of the Lewinsky story, conservative demands that, as *Post* columnist Steve Dunleavy put it, feminists "ravage Clinton the same way they ravaged Clarence Thomas" went into high gear.

Undeterred that Lewinsky had been over twenty-one during the (then still alleged) affair and had not complained of harassment or indeed complained at all, right-wing champions pronounced her a victim of at best exploitation, at worst child-molesting. Where they would ordinarily have been inclined to see Monica as a nutty/slutty temptress and condemnation of her male partner as a case of totalitarian sexual correctness, they had now evidently adopted the view of the correctniks that sex between a woman and her boss, or between a young woman and a powerful older man, is inherently abusive. Kathleen Willey's claim that she was groped in the White House, with its echoes of Bob Packwood, was a more plausible subject of indignation, but since Lewinsky was the focus of Kenneth Starr's inquiry and the public's attention, conservatives showed little interest in distinguishing her case from

Willey's or even Jones's: the three were simply lumped together as "Clinton's women." In their zeal to portray the president as the worst serial abuser of women since Bluebeard, some even tossed Gennifer Flowers into the mix of victims, despite her publicly voiced admiration for Bill's talents as a lover (on a scale of 1 to 10, she rated him a 9). Feminists, they insisted, were duty-bound to support Starr's investigation: if they really believed that the personal is political, their partisan loyalties to Clinton and the Democrats would not deter them from defending their sisters.

Their own hypocrisy aside, the conservatives' logic was faulty. To assert that "the personal is political" is to claim that politics is not synonymous with government but extends to those sexual and domestic relations in which men exercise institutionalized power over women. It doesn't necessarily follow that "personal politics" should be feminists' chief criterion for judging a public official—that who he is as a sexual actor should outweigh who he is as an agent of the state. This is not to say that a male politician's personal relations with women are inherently irrelevant to his office (as many of Clinton's defenders have argued), but rather that except in cases clearly involving violence or abuse, there is no inconsistency in arguing that other issues—the politician's public stance and policies on women's rights, the motivation and political agenda of his enemies—are more important. Such trade-offs are, after all, the essence of electoral politics, which normally is not about purity of principle but about compromise and lesser-evilism. The last time this question came up for feminists was in 1980, when Ted Kennedy ran against Jimmy Carter in the Democratic presidential primary: the womanizer with a staunch pro-woman record in the Senate versus the apparently faithful spouse who had distanced his administration from the women's movement and opposed federal funding for abortion. My position then was "Marry Carter; vote for Kennedy."

Clinton's situation doesn't lend itself to one-liners. His reputation as a pro-feminist president is, on the level of policy, mostly myth. Though he has appointed women to high-level positions and defended abortion, he has also pandered shamelessly to the family-values sentiments of cultural conservatives—especially their campaign against "illegitimacy" —and signed a welfare "reform" bill whose essence is an attack on impoverished single mothers; nor does his fidelity to corporate economic priorities benefit women as a group. But as a cultural figure, he evokes the revisionist masculinity of his generation with his soft, sensual, semi-androgynous sexual persona, his avoidance of military service, and his egalitarian marriage. (Indeed, for most of his time in office criticism of his personal life centered less on his alleged affairs than on his refusal to put Hillary in her place.) The far right's single-minded hatred and determination to bring Clinton down has been driven not by his quasi-Republican program but by outrage that such a figure should have attained either the political power or the symbolic authority attached to the presidency. From this choleric standpoint, the Lewinsky scandal merely confirmed that the Oval Office had become, as Pat Robertson put it, "the playpen for the sexual freedom of the poster child of the 1960's."

The Lewinsky witch hunt was at its core an effort to crush the perceived cultural enemy by any means necessary and plant the flag of patriarchal morality on the corpse. It began with the victimization of Lewinsky, not by Clinton but by Linda Tripp, who illegally taped her phone calls, and by Starr, who used those illegally obtained tapes as an excuse to entrap her and threaten her with prosecution unless she delivered the goods. Starr went on to mobilize a terrifying array of hardball tactics, amplified by the independent counsel's virtually unlimited license to pursue a long-running, open-ended fishing expedition aimed at one suspect—in the process raising troubling questions about the independent counsel statute and the power of federal prosecutors even when directed at "deserving" targets like mob bosses—all to unmask a consensual affair between two adults and the lies meant to conceal it. It was hardly in the interest of feminists to sign on to a crusade that subverted civil liberties and turned the screws on a woman whose major "crime" was terminal lack of discretion (or woefully insufficient paranoia) in order to destroy a president for his real and imagined sexual liberalism.

As for Jones, there were reasons other than bigotry against trailer park residents to be skeptical of her story. One important way it differed from Hill's was simply that Hill's already existed: the Thomas-Hill affair had provided at once a model of how to make trouble for a political enemy and a means of embarrassing feminists—a doubly tempting motive for Clinton haters to prevail on Jones to invent, or more likely edit, her story of an encounter with the governor. Then there was the matter—intangible, to be sure, but assessing someone's credibility often hinges on intangibles—of one's sense of Bill Clinton as a sexual animal. I could imagine John F. Kennedy, who appears to have had a blanket contempt for wife and girlfriends alike, having the droit-du-seigneur mentality to behave as Jones alleged. But Clinton has never conveyed the impression of misogyny or unquestioned confidence in his right to dominate. On the contrary, he is insecure. He wants to please, to charm; and the drop-trou scenario is anything but charming. Although Jones may nonetheless have been telling the truth—as with Thomas and Hill, we will never really know—she did not compel belief.

Yet while most feminists intuitively understood that it was Starr's inquisition they should be worried about, not Clinton's libido, the efforts of the liberal feminist establishment to articulate that view were unconvincing. Like the rest of what passes for the left, feminist organizations and politicians had by January 1998 long since forfeited their claim to an independent voice and circled their wagons around the administration. Had they even once rebelled against Clinton—say, organized public protests and threatened to withdraw their support if he signed the infamous welfare bill—they would have been less vulnerable to the charge of knee-jerk partisanship in the Lewinsky crisis; but they hadn't. When the news broke, their first impulse was to make cautionary noises about rushing to judgment. But that response not only sounded fake—who, after reading the excerpts from Tripp's tapes, could say with a straight face that they believed Clinton when he denied having sex with "that woman"?—it seemed to concede that if he had, his behavior was indeed comparable to what Thomas was alleged to have done; and if that were true, why weren't feminists demonstrating in front of the White House, demanding that the president explain himself and cooperate fully with the independent counsel?

The next line of defense was to suggest that, as Gloria Steinem put it in a *New York Times* op-ed, Clinton's alleged actions fell within feminists' "common sense guideline to sexual behavior . . . no means no; yes means yes." The problem here was that so many feminists for so long had argued that in a male-dominated society, no meant no, but yes could mean something more ambiguous. In any case, this line applied better to Lewinsky than to Willey or (especially) Jones. Steinem argued that if Willey and Jones were to be believed, in both cases the president had simply "made a clumsy sexual pass, then accepted rejection." Willey's alleged groping might fit that description (though you would have to add the word "pushy," at the very least). But Jones's story? For the CEO to summon an employee he's never met and, without any preliminaries to speak of, ask her to kiss his dick is no more a "pass," a word that implies some vague connection to ordinary conventions of courtship, than the same request coming from a furtive, glassy-eyed guy in the subway— though it is, I would imagine, more intimidating.

In the wake of the firestorm after Clinton's August confession, many establishment feminists, sharing the political panic of the Democrats and worn down by constant criticism, denounced the president's behavior as morally reprehensible, while still refusing conservatives' demands that they repudiate him as a misogynist and call for his resignation. Trying to present themselves as independent yet judicious, they succeeded mainly in sounding ever more defensive and incoherent. For at bottom, liberal feminists' problem was not simply a matter of blind loyalty; it reflected deep confusions and contradictions in feminist thinking. The Lewinsky scandal had sprung a trap that was set when the dictum "the personal is political" devolved from a tool of social analysis to a weapon of moral condemnation. For its coiners, the idea was that the social rules governing sex, marriage, and motherhood were part of a system that enforced women's subordination, so that much of what appeared to individual women to be their own private unhappiness was widely shared and reflected their social inequality. Armed with that knowledge, women could demand changes in the rules. But over the years, the slogan has increasingly come to mean that all personal behavior is subject to political judgment, that there are now feminist rules both sexes should obey. Accordingly, feminism, insofar as it deals with personal life, has largely abandoned politics, which seeks to affect social structures, for moralism, which aims to control individuals.

Like all moral crusaders, the feminist kind are impatient with the argument that people can't simply change their sexual psychology at will. Nor does consent count: if a woman chooses to condone a man's bad behavior, she is either guilty of collaboration or a victim whether she admits it or not. By this logic, a president who fools around with a White House intern should be in big trouble. After all, such behavior replicates one of the culture's hardier sexist clichés: the powerful older man amusing himself with a sexy woman whose youth, inexperience, lack of worldly clout, and awe of him feed his ego. (In the bargain, one can't help suspecting Bill of seeking a little relief from having to live up to that egalitarian marriage—and of rebelling against Hillary's moral authority by being a bad boy.) But the logic is screwy. Given the president's importance as a cultural icon, it would clearly be nicer for feminism if he'd had an affair with, say, Barbra Streisand; but does it actually further the cause of sexual equality to define gender-stereotyped erotic tastes as an impeachable offense? Was watching the president's downfall supposed to inspire the millions of people in relationships based on the mutual lust (sometimes even love) of young women and powerful men to change their ways? Is it the business of feminism to condemn and where possible punish such couples? Perhaps we should get on the case of men who reveal their sexism *and* racism by their tropism for thin women with blond hair?

If feminist moralism were applied to any area other than sex—housework, for instance—its absurdity would be apparent: imagine trying to make a political scandal of the fact that most male politicians spend little time at home and dump all domestic responsibilities on their wives. But in fact its central purpose has always been sexual repression; it arose from certain feminists' conviction that sex is fundamentally a male weapon for subjugating women. The right understands all this a lot better than liberal feminists, who, having swallowed the moral reading of "the personal is political," found themselves groping for arguments about why it didn't apply in this case.

The right also knows what it thinks about sex, while mainstream feminism is thoroughly ambivalent and confused on the subject. Its dominant impulse—especially among academic and corporate bureaucrats—is, as feminist anthropologist Gayle Rubin once remarked, to presume that sex is guilty till proven innocent (and in our litigious era that's no mere metaphor). Not only has the antisexual strain in feminist politics—particularly as it has been expressed through antipornography and antisexual harassment activism—been a powerful influence; the pervasiveness of "pro-family" cultural conservatism, even in feminist circles, has spread the idea that any departure from monogamy is inherently antiwoman. Yet there is also a vocal contingent of feminists who oppose the sexual moralists, arguing that sexual freedom is integral to women's equality. And since liberal feminism, like liberalism in general, goes where it's pushed, the pro-sex influence has made itself felt, at least to the extent of prodding the movement's spokespeople to extend their "right to choose" rhetoric from abortion to sex itself. These competing sets of ideas float around in the thin gruel of an orthodox feminist conversation largely devoid of real political content, available to be fished out and brandished when they seem to fit the occasion. I don't mean that Steinem was insincere when she said "no means no; yes means yes." It's just that she acted as if large chunks of feminist history, in which she herself had been involved, simply didn't exist.

Still another dilemma for Clinton's feminist defenders, especially in the matter of Paula Jones, was squaring their stance with an entrenched item of conventional movement wisdom—that since men have notoriously gotten away with all manner of crimes against women by vilifying them as liars, feminists must redress the balance by assuming that men always lie and women always tell the truth. This assumption is silly; but because it has deep roots in women's collective expe-

rience of having their reality denied, it is not easily relinquished. Given the highly charged atmosphere surrounding
Clarence Thomas's nomination, it was not unreasonable for
his advocates to worry that an opposition about to lose the
battle might resort to dirty tricks. Yet when Republican senators and other partisans attacked Anita Hill's credibility,
many feminists were incensed not only at the misogynist and
often bizarre character of the attacks—or at the lack of evidence for the feminist cabal that was darkly alleged—but at
the fact that her truthfulness should be questioned at all. This
precedent enabled conservatives to profess shock that feminists would not embrace Jones's tale, no questions asked—especially about the political agenda of her sponsors. One result, it seems to me, is the tortured reasoning in Steinem's
piece. I suspect that she didn't believe Jones's account any
more than I did, but that having accepted its truth "for the
sake of argument," she felt compelled to deny its seriousness.

As the foregoing observations suggest, much of the murk
that afflicted feminists' response to the Lewinsky scandal can
be traced to precisely that larger-than-life episode that cast
its shadow over Clinton's troubles: the Anita Hill–Clarence
Thomas confrontation. Indeed, feminists' difficulty in an-
swering the challenge, "Why go after Thomas and not Clinton?" ultimately has less to do with Clinton than with
Thomas. The iconic status of the Thomas-Hill affair, and of
Anita Hill as a feminist heroine, has discouraged second
thoughts. It was, after all, the event that put sexual harassment
on the political map. And as public opinion shifted toward
Hill in the aftermath of Thomas's confirmation, feminists felt
powerfully vindicated: this moral victory, in the face of political defeat, showed that a woman could be believed when she
accused a powerful man of abuse, and that—in the face of
Thomas's "high-tech lynching" speech and the accusation by
many blacks that Hill was a tool of white feminists—a black

woman could successfully challenge the idea that it was dis-
loyal to the race to call an abusive black man to account. Yet
the legacy of this triumphant moment has been decidedly ambiguous — and in some ways disastrous.

The original outcry on behalf of Anita Hill was not only, or
even primarily, about sexual harassment. It erupted as it did
for a simmering stew of reasons. There was feminists' desperation over the alliance of the Reagan and Bush administra-
tions with the Christian right and the imminent appointment
of a right-wing ideologue to the Supreme Court, at a time
when it was widely assumed that one more antiabortion vote
would topple *Roe v. Wade*. There was the smug protectiveness
of the old boys in the Senate. And there was above all the
decade-long, cumulative frustration of women in a political
atmosphere that increasingly denied the legitimacy of their
anger at men. The "they" in that iconic rallying cry, "They just
don't get it!" did not refer simply to the misguided senators
but to men in general; "it" was not just Hill's complaint but
the sum total of unheeded, invalidated female complaints
about the whole range of oppressive male behavior women
had to put up with — in short, the culture of male dominance.
At that moment "they" were the object not only of rage but of
cynicism and even hatred: as feminist social critic Judith Levine suggested in a book published a year later, the unspoken
coda to "They don't get it" is "and they never will, those hopeless assholes!"

Conservatives never did get this key aspect of the pro-Hill
revolt. They insisted that the outpouring of female fury was a
media campaign orchestrated by feminist organizations, and
in a sense they were right. But feminists had not been able to
foment such a reaction on other issues — abortion rights, for
instance — and not for lack of trying. All the orchestration
they could muster would not have produced a national obsession had Hill not hit a larger cultural nerve. (For this reason,

the right's effort to promote Paula Jones as Anita Hill II was not only opportunistic but tin-eared. Even if organized feminism had been assiduous in coming to Jones's defense, the issue would not have ignited: aside from the second-time-around problem, the iconography was all wrong. Clinton's sexual persona and his general pliability—not to mention the diminished aura of the presidency in an age of corporate rule—made him an unsuitable figure on which to project free-floating rage at male power. Nor was it possible to make a convincing feminist heroine of a woman who was being used by right-wingers against a man they hated in large part because they saw him as a traitor to masculinist culture.)

Yet for those who were listening carefully, the reaction to Thomas-Hill exposed a troubling distortion in the public conversation about feminism. The thought that something about the furor didn't quite track first occurred to me in connection with Levine's book, *My Enemy, My Love*. Appearing at a time when Thomas and Hill were still the subject of hot and bitter emotion, it was a brave attempt to write honestly about man-hating, that taboo emotion—feared by men, anxiously denied by women, routinely projected onto feminists—that was in fact a powerful if usually subterranean strain in the female psyche, an ongoing emotional protest against the sexism of everyday life. The book's original subtitle was *Man-hating and Ambivalence in Women's Lives;* but when the paperback edition came out, I noticed that it had been sanitized to *Women, Men, and the Dilemmas of Gender.* According to Levine, The Word had been a total conversation stopper: people either refused to go near the book (as if it harbored a contagious disease) or substituted their fantasy of what the author must be saying for her actual, impeccably humanist perspective. Odd, isn't it? An author dares to put the word "man-hating" on a book jacket and reviewers and potential readers go berserk, convinced they are being stalked by some killer dyke out of the movie *Basic Instinct* — even as a dramatic outburst of what could reasonably be called man-hating, channeled through the issue of sexual harassment, is taken quite seriously and acclaimed, not only by feminists but by male commentators and editorial writers, as a long overdue national teach-in, mass consciousness-raising session, and so on.

In fact, this schizophrenia had been a long time in the making. At a feminist meeting I attended in the mid-'70s, a member of the group wondered, "Why all of a sudden is the movement so preoccupied with violence? Why have feminists stopped talking about mundane kinds of sexism, like your husband constantly interrupts you or 'forgets' when it's his turn to do the shopping?" Someone else pointed out that in feminist discussion about sex, the emphasis had changed from confronting men with their petty tyrannies in the bedroom — the myriad small acts of selfishness, ignorance, and egotism that interfered with women's sexual pleasure — to denouncing rape as the paradigm for male power. In retrospect it's clear that we were witnessing a pivotal moment in the movement's history: as the women's revolution hit a wall of reaction, many feminists' utopian hopes gave way to despair. From then on radical feminism, whose most distinctive contribution had been critiquing the sexist patterns embedded in male-female relations, was increasingly influenced by its separatist fringe and came to connote, to the public as well as to many of the activists themselves, a rejection of heterosexuality as inherently abusive. After all, you could demand that your husband share the housework or be a more sensitive lover, but if he hit or raped you, what was there to do but throw him out and have him locked up?

These observations are even more apt today. One of the great successes of the antifeminist reaction is that there is now no socially acceptable public language in which women, particularly young women, can directly and explicitly express anger at the "mundane kinds of sexism," or what I've called the sexism of everyday life—that is, men's ubiquitous, culturally sanctioned, "normal" expressions of dominance. To be sure, such expressions are documented in a large body of pop-psychological/sociological literature; but, as in Deborah Tannen's best-selling *You Just Don't Understand,* they are presented as neutral cultural differences that hinder communication between the sexes—not as strategies, however reflexive or unconscious, for preserving male power. To suggest that the source of chronic, common-cold-level male-female conflict is not misunderstanding but inequality is to invite the quarantine reflex that greeted Levine's book. Yet women have been deeply influenced by feminism; they desperately want men to "get it"; and they are furious. Where are these feelings to go?

At first it seemed that the eruption over Thomas-Hill might reopen a long-suppressed discussion. Men reacted, for a while at least, with a degree of self-consciousness, defensiveness, and worry about their own behavior ("Is it okay to tell a woman she looks nice today?") unknown since the launching of radical feminism some twenty years earlier. And sexual harassment is easily related to more general patterns of sexism: the assumption that men have the right to define the sexual norms women must conform to; the corollary assumption that men's view of what goes on between men and women is reality, while contrary views expressed by women are oversensitive, dishonest, vindictive, or crazy; men's frequent predatory and manipulative behavior in pursuing sex and disregard of women's signals that their attention is unwanted; men's reluctance to accept women's presence in the public world as workers, citizens, even mere pedestrians, rather than as objects of their sexual assessment or desire.

To some extent that larger discussion did take place—especially in black feminists' analyses of the case as a crossroads of racial and sexual politics—but it was mostly confined to academic circles. In the mass media the taboo on admitting how mundane, pervasive, and *normal* sexism is remained stubbornly in force. Rather than stimulating a broad critique of male-female relations as such, the hearings entered popular discourse as a riveting morality tale of Hill the long-suffering martyr versus Thomas the sexual predator, encouraging women to encode their anger in the limited vocabulary of sexual victimization and abuse. In effect, the Thomas-Hill affair became the vehicle for bringing into the mainstream the shift that had already occurred within radical feminism, from understanding sexual violence and harassment as particularly blatant excrescences of a sexist culture to seeing violence as the essential fact of sexism.

From this perspective, all manifestations of sexism are forms of violence, and feminist consciousness-raising means combating public resistance to admitting the extent of violence against women. "Violence" is thereby robbed of all concreteness and becomes a metaphor for a larger, and largely inexpressible, set of feminist concerns. The complexities of male-female relations—those tensions of enmity and love that Judith Levine was trying to explore—are flattened to caricatures of villains and victims; the radical demand for equality in personal life is displaced onto a profoundly conservative appeal for law and order. While daily grievances remain unanalyzed, uncontested, and unredressed, women soothe their anger with the fantasy that men's refusal to "get it" can be outlawed and punished.

So long as sexism remains the dominant culture—ingrained in the texture of people's everyday behavior, language, imagery, thought, feeling—that fantasy is at once totalitarian and absurd. Yet it has had a serious political result: campaigns to stretch the meaning of rape and sexual harassment to cover a wide range of male sexual behavior that a woman may find unwelcome or offensive. Antirape activists want to blur the legal line between physically forcing a woman to have sex, or threatening her with force, and subjecting her to verbal and psychological pressure. The term sexual harassment is increasingly used to refer not only to specific uses of sex that interfere with women's ability to work or inhabit public space, but to male-dominated or male-oriented sexual culture per se—which in turn is increasingly conflated with sex itself.

The agenda of sexual harassment politics, post Thomas-Hill, can basically be traced to one key figure: Catharine MacKinnon, the chief feminist architect of sexual harassment law, who is also a leading exponent of the idea that pornography is violence against women. Since the villain-victim model of sexual politics cannot, by definition, grant women any dimension of autonomy or pleasure in their sexual relations with men, it inevitably reduces those relations to rape: the antipornography movement takes this equation a convolution further, defining as violence not only heterosexual acts but sexual desire, fantasy, and representation. In a fateful convergence of MacKinnon's central concerns, the case that was to become, in the public mind, synonymous with sexual harassment happened to hinge on a woman's allegations of verbal smuttiness against a man who was reportedly fond of pornographic magazines, films, and videos. (Though Thomas's supposed taste for pornography was arguably germane to his credibility, since it contradicted his claim to share Hill's distaste for sexually explicit language, it proved nothing about how he had behaved toward her—a distinction rarely made by his detractors.)

As a result, the issue of sexual harassment has come to be viewed chiefly through the lens of the antiporn movement, with its assumption that any form of sexual expression in the workplace subjects women to the "intimidating, hostile, or offensive" environment proscribed by federal law. In universities, charges of sexual harassment have become a rubric for promoting censorship and undermining academic freedom: a male professor is accused of using a sexual comparison to make a point in class; a teaching assistant, supported by her professor, warns a student she considers him a harasser for handing in a paper containing an "inappropriate" sexual analogy; the State Board of Regents orders professors at the University of Iowa to warn students before exposing them to sexually explicit material. There is also a growing trend toward defining as sexual harassment consensual sex between men and their female students or subordinates and invoking that definition to justify banning or punishing such relationships. Indeed, current sexual harassment law admits a defendant's consensual affairs with subordinates as evidence of a pattern of behavior supporting the charge of harassment—which is how Bill Clinton came to be deposed about Monica Lewinsky in the first place. While it's not unreasonable to suggest that a boss's or professor's affair with someone whose work he (or she) is directly supervising can pose problems —conflict of interest, potential favoritism, and so on—it's another matter to infantilize women by claiming that they are incapable of choosing whether or not to sleep with more powerful men.

That Anita Hill's trauma has been put to such dubious uses raises a question most feminists would prefer to consider settled: assuming that Hill told the truth—and I too am inclined to believe she did—was Thomas's behavior sexual harassment? That is (and here I'll try to formulate my own definition of the slippery beast), was it a systematic effort to interfere with Hill's work by treating her as an erotic object or extension of his sexual fantasy world rather than as a colleague? Was it a way of punishing Hill for taking her job seriously, of putting her in her place by constantly reminding her in the crudest possible way that they were not only boss and subordinate but man and (mere) woman? Or was Thomas simply an obnoxious, angry guy who no doubt sensed Hill's vulnerability and enjoyed baiting her, but was not engaged in a campaign to sabotage her work?

Listening to Hill's rendition of Thomas's words and actions—abstracted from their original context, his tone of voice, his body language—I couldn't tell. Nor did it help to read the endless reporting and commentary on Thomas (including Jane Mayer and Jill Abramson's *Strange Justice*, which made the most convincing case for believing Hill's testimony). Had Hill been a plaintiff in a lawsuit, able to subject Thomas to cross-examination and call all relevant witnesses, would we have gotten a clearer picture? To some extent, perhaps; but in the end this kind of behavior is inherently ambiguous and subject to interpretation.

Am I then comfortable with the idea of a man with this level of sexual hostility, even if it's not legally actionable, sitting on the Supreme Court? Well, no, I'm not. But before Hill came into the picture, I was already opposed to Thomas's appointment on the grounds of his right-wing politics, which —despite his strategic refusal to answer questions about abortion—were not ambiguous in the least; and the same is undoubtedly true of every feminist who demanded that Hill be heard. How would I feel if a prospective justice with an expansive view of women's civil rights were similarly accused? Immediately the distinction I'd found so hard to make in Thomas's case would become crucially important. For if the man was a true sexual harasser—in the habit of using sex as a weapon to subvert women's right to equal treatment in the workplace—he was unfit to be a judge. But if he was just a sexist jerk, who managed like so many men to disconnect his noble public principles about women's equality from his piggish personal relations — or if it wasn't clear, as it probably wouldn't be, which category he fell into — I would be inclined to decide that it was in women's best interest to give the noble public principles the nod.

Similarly, I'm convinced that feminism would have been better served if the opposition to Thomas had remained focused on his legal and political philosophy. By becoming the dramatic center of the confirmation hearings, the Thomas-Hill confrontation legitimized and promoted the idea that feminists should judge public figures chiefly on their personal behavior toward women, even as the MacKinnonites' co-optation of the drama would promote a dangerously loose conception of sexual harassment and abuse. Furthermore, when Hill became the issue that would decide Thomas's fate, a battle over political ideas was supplanted by a clash between different versions of reality — compounded by uncertainty about what Hill's version might mean — that could never be definitively resolved. It is this history that has enabled the right to claim a feminist moral imprimatur for Starr's exercise. Worse, it has played a crucial part in creating the repressive climate that made such a travesty possible.

Postscript: This book was already in type when Juanita Broaddrick's allegation that Bill Clinton raped her in 1978 surfaced in the mainstream press. Ironically, though her story is the most serious charge of sexually abusive behavior yet leveled against Clinton, it will no doubt get the least attention. Perhaps that's as it should be, with charges that are twenty years old and probably impossible to prove. Yet the irony underscores how little the prevailing rhetoric about sexual harassment and abuse has to do with the thing itself. For a year the Republicans cried wolf, attacking Clinton on the basis of feminists' worst confusions between consensual and coercive sex. As a result, the public is in no mood to listen to further accusations, and anti-impeachment Republican Senator Jim Jeffords feels free to dismiss an alleged rape as a private matter. Progress, anyone?

'Tis Pity He's a Whore

As Bill Clinton looked me straight in the eye, tightened his jaw, and denied having sexual relations with "that woman," I had a fantasy: suppose, on that historic *60 Minutes* episode in 1992, he had said, "Yes, I had an affair with Gennifer Flowers." And suppose Hillary had added, "Not every marriage is monogamous. Relationships are complicated, and ours is no exception."

Why is such candor unthinkable? After all, most of the voters who elected Clinton didn't believe his denial that he'd slept with Flowers, any more than they would believe his denial about Monica Lewinsky, five and a half years and a second victorious campaign later. There's a good chance that Americans would have supported the Clintons' right to set the terms of their marriage — even identified with it, considering the complications of their own lives. Yet declining to tell the lies that pay homage to virtue would indeed have been a daring political gamble and a shocking, radical act. It would instantly have shifted the debate from whether personal lapses from conservative sexual and familial values should disqualify a candidate for public office to a more basic issue: should public officials be required to conform to those values in the first place? Bill Clinton, who is neither a radical nor much of a political gambler, was not about to stake his candidacy on the outcome of such a debate. But by lying, he acceded to his opponents' moral framework. Had he challenged it and won anyway, he would have done himself and the entire country a favor by showing that politicians, even presidents, need no longer submit to the sexual blackmail of the right. Instead, he supplied the rope that has strangled his presidency.

My enthusiasm for radical candor won't sit well with those who argue that the worst feature of the presidential scandal was its contribution to a horrifying breakdown of the distinction between public and private life. Jean Cohen and Andrew Arato—responding in *Dissent* to the article where I first made the foregoing suggestion—contend that the proper public response to intrusive sexual questions is simply that they are "out of line and nobody's business." Of course, Clinton shouldn't have to discuss his sex life with the media. Nor should he have been questioned about a consensual affair in a sexual harassment lawsuit, any more than a woman who complains of sexual harassment should have to testify about her sexual relationships with other men in the office. Nor should Kenneth Starr have been allowed to investigate Clinton's relationship with Lewinsky on the pretext that his attempt to cover up an affair he shouldn't have been asked about in the first place was relevant to the Whitewater inquiry. Nor should Starr have forced Lewinsky to testify by threatening to prosecute her and her mother on the basis of illegal tapes, or asked her questions about the minute details of her encounters with the president, ostensibly to nail down Clinton's perjury but actually to strip him naked before the world. Nor should the House have voted to release this material to the public, with utter disregard for what is supposed to be the confidentiality of grand jury proceedings (granted that Starr's leaks to the press had long since made it a joke). Clearly what we have witnessed is the frightening spectacle of right-wing zealots abusing the power of the state to invade Clinton's—and Lewinsky's—privacy.

But public discussion of what to make of this invasion has displayed a persistent confusion—shared by queasy liberal commentators and ambivalent "ordinary Americans" alike—

between sexual privacy and sexual secrecy. The two are in fact very different in their meaning and purpose. Genuine sexual privacy rests on the belief that consensual sexual behavior is a matter of individual liberty that need not and ought not be policed. Privacy will be consistently respected only in a sexually libertarian culture, for repression inevitably gives rise to a prurient preoccupation with other people's sex lives. And when privacy is respected, secrecy is unnecessary: as the actor and libertarian Orson Bean once observed, if people were brought up in a culture where eating was considered a shameful act, they might rebel against that social taboo, yet they could never truly imagine the unselfconsciousness of Americans dining in a restaurant.

Secrecy, on the other hand, is based on the need to hide one's behavior from public scrutiny and judgment. What's at stake is not only moral respectability but dignity, in a culture where sexual needs and appetites are still on some level regarded as infantile, ridiculous, and an offense to our higher spiritual natures. The widespread acceptance of secrecy ("everybody lies about sex") reflects the recognition that people must protect themselves from others' prurience; but it's also a way to avoid openly confronting the gap between our official standards of morality and dignity and our actual behavior. While the defense of privacy involves a critique of conservative sexual norms, the defense of secrecy serves to enforce them by denying their ubiquitous violation. Refusing secrecy, and the shame it implies, can paradoxically further the cause of privacy. A person's sexual orientation, for instance, is surely nobody's business. Yet by choosing to come out of the closet, often in the most public of ways, gay and lesbian activists launched us on the path toward a society in which homosexuals may enjoy their private lives without constant fear of exposure and punishment.

When the Lewinsky story broke, media commentators indulged in such an outpouring of nostalgia for the good old days of "Don't ask, don't tell"—before those feminists decided that the personal is political and oral sex made it onto *Nightline*—that you would have thought judging politicians' private lives was something new. On the contrary, candidates, especially for the presidency, have always been vetted by the family-values cops for marital respectability. Until Ronald Reagan broke the taboo, no divorced man had ever become president. (I always admired Nelson Rockefeller for divorcing his wife to marry the woman he loved, though it probably meant the end of his presidential prospects.) Open homosexuality is still beyond the pale, as is heterosexual cohabiting out of wedlock. Presidential wives are supposed to be supportive mates, preferably mothers, domestic minded, and never openly sexual.

What *is* new is the end of the trade-off that allowed politicians, in return for outward conformity, to lead a secret sexual life on the side. This conspiracy of silence, joined by the press, served to maintain strict public norms and the illusion that authority figures exemplified the morality they preached, while cutting powerful men some slack. (Needless to say, the deal has never been available to female candidates or political wives.) It also mystified sex, keeping the gritty details of respectable men's disreputable desires and practices from compromising the enforced "innocence" (that is, ignorance) of respectable women and children. The undoing of this corrupt bargain is part of our society's continuing revolt against Victorian morality, sexual hypocrisy, and a sexist double standard. From this perspective, open discussion of the realities of people's sex lives—including the sex lives of public figures—is much to be preferred. If revelations of politicians' sexual proclivities cripple their ability to indulge in pious blather about the evils of "illegitimacy," I can only cheer.

Yet this assault on repression, however desirable in the

long historical view, has given rise to an immediate and serious problem: while sexual secrecy has broken down, sexual privacy has yet to be achieved. In these circumstances, the readiness of the media to pass along sexual revelations becomes a weapon of outraged moralists bent on restoring the old sexual order. And ironically, the loudest defenders of secrecy are likely, once it has collapsed, to end up joining the hunt. For if the norms can no longer be upheld by concealment, then they must be upheld by punishment, and if necessary by purge. It is this imperative that explains the curious reversal of the nation's journalistic and political establishment, from its initial horror that the president's sex life should be exposed in the national media and investigated by the independent counsel to the outpouring of high moral indignation that followed Clinton's grudging confession of an "inappropriate relationship." The underlying theme remained the same: the moral authority of the president and the presidency must be preserved—an authority presumed to require an acceptable facade of sexual dignity and "family values."

There was a surreal quality to the revulsion and, even more peculiar, the sense of betrayal that Clinton's speech unleashed among Democratic politicians, administration officials, and the standard-bearers of what I think of as "high journalism"—that is, the (mostly moderate conservative to neoliberal) commentators for the major dailies and TV networks, including the editorialists of the *New York Times.* In the weeks leading up to the president's grand jury testimony, the prevailing line in these circles was that Clinton should publicly admit and apologize for the Lewinsky affair; that the admission could not hurt him since hardly anyone believed him anyway; that the country simply wanted to hear the truth, after which it could achieve "closure" and "move on." But as it turned out, for this same crowd there was all the difference in the world between believing the president had lied and hearing him confirm the fact. The aides and politicians who had loyally echoed Clinton's denials now felt compelled, whatever the insult to everyone's intelligence, to declare their shock. Centrist Democrats in Congress—led by Senator Joseph Lieberman, whose last claim to fame had been a moral crusade against TV talk shows—saw yet another chance to "take the values issue away from the right." And the high journalists, who resented the saturation coverage of the sex scandal as the latest affront to their role as guardians of serious public discourse (in their worldview, sex is much too interesting to be legitimate news), turned that resentment from Starr and the tabloids toward the man whose behavior, by his own admission, had made the media orgy possible.

In short, the moment the secret was really out, the logic of preserving moral authority demanded that Clinton somehow manage to say something so powerfully redemptive that he would in effect be born again, shedding his tainted public persona for a new one worthy of the presidential mantle. The specific complaints against the president's speech—that he wasn't abject enough, that he attacked Starr, that he continued to weasel out of admitting perjury—reflected a larger frustration with his failure to accomplish what even for a gifted politician was an impossible task. No apology, made under extreme duress by an admitted liar with a long-term reputation for philandering, could have sufficed; and Clinton's subsequent attempts to juice up his repentance were merely embarrassing. Soon a chorus of voices—among them the *Times* and both Democratic congressional leaders—began suggesting that the president could yet appease his critics by giving up his last shred of cover (not to mention his legal right to defend himself against a criminal charge) and confessing that he lied under oath. If Clinton had fallen for that one, he would have been as pathetic as Charlie Brown perennially kicking the football because Lucy swears that this time she won't pull it away at the last minute.

The logical resolution of the demand that the president magically turn into someone else was resignation or impeachment. And indeed, even as Starr and the congressional Republicans were doing everything they could to ensure that Clinton's image was defined by cigar-fucking and dress stains, while Democrats cowered in fear of being associated with "immorality," growing numbers of high journalists and elder-statespeople types hinted or openly suggested that the president spare our sensibilities by stepping down. The logic might have been irresistible, if it had not hit a major snag: the public's refusal to get with the program.

Commentators who have attributed Americans' lack of lynch-mob fervor to a "Who cares, the economy's good" attitude illuminate little but their own condescension (and their membership in that minority for whom the economy actually *is* good). Conservatives like William Bennett, who mourn "the death of outrage," are closer to the mark. In fact, the electorate's feelings about Clinton mirror the contemporary standoff in the culture wars, both on the issue of sexual morality and on the larger question of how we view authority. On the one hand, most people believe, or profess to believe, that Clinton's behavior with Lewinsky was morally wrong; yet they are also strongly influenced by the idea of a right to free sexual association between consenting adults. They are unhappy with his lies, but think the questions that provoked them should not have been asked. They would have preferred to fudge the contradictions with secrecy, but are reluctant to deny the president privacy—and on both counts are leery of the right's moral police.

Even more telling, perhaps, "ordinary" Americans clearly do not share the Washington elite's investment in the idea of the president as a moral exemplar, charged with validating the existing structure of (patriarchal) authority. They see him as a man elected to do a job, a politician in a political culture where lies are a taken-for-granted part of the game and sex is a perk of power. It's hardly news that the public's respect for the governing class and the establishment press is not at an all-time high. For those once accustomed to deference, its loss is an ongoing crisis, which the Lewinsky scandal exacerbated to an intolerable degree: as they see it, "cynicism" threatens to undermine democracy, unless the elite gets its house in order. Yet in fact Americans' refusal to put their "leaders" on a pedestal is not only eminently democratic, but altogether realistic, in an age when the nation-state is steadily weakening and the president, as Stanley Aronowitz has put it, is basically a trade representative.

Nor is this refusal merely cynical; it also involves an element of identification. The Republican strategy of bombarding the public with sexual details fizzled, not only because people saw it as gratuitous and hypocritical, but because it shifted the focus of moral disapproval from the fact of Clinton's sexual relationship with Lewinsky to the nature of their activities. In the wake of the Starr Report, the *New York Post* pronounced its revelations "kinky"; *Post* columnist John Podhoretz bragged of his superior character on the grounds that he had never used a cigar for sexual purposes or been sexually serviced while on the phone; Congressmen lamented the disgrace of it all; and even the president's lawyers, complaining about the report, called its sexual descriptions "lurid." All this huffing and puffing was bound to make people nervous, inspiring discomfiting thoughts about how lurid or kinky their own sexual impulses and quirks might look in front of an audience. Nobody, after all, is a moral authority while having sex, even with one's spouse in the missionary position under the covers. In any case, the Bill Clinton of the Starr Report does not come across as an arrogant exploiter, a Sadeian libertine, the creepy exhibitionist depicted by Paula Jones. Rather, he seems needy, affectionate, attracted yet painfully cautious and conflicted, and terrified of getting caught—in short, a neurotic middle-aged married guy, ordinary to the point of banality, except that he happens to be president of the United States. That most people saw no need to get rid of him on that account speaks well for their acceptance of their own sexuality.

If it's true that Dick Morris's poll results convinced Clinton he had to lie to the public about Lewinsky, this was a fateful miscalculation, seemingly at odds with his usual political instincts. But it's consistent with a long-standing contradiction in the president's modus operandi. Bill Clinton was elected in large part because of who he was: a member of the '60s generation, an embodiment of youth and eroticism. To be sure, he was on the clean-cut, respectable end of the spectrum of '60s types, a man who from the beginning had had mainstream political ambitions. Yet there were certain influences he couldn't help inhaling: his style and body language bore the imprint of shaggy hair, rock and roll, the sexual revolution, the blurring of racial and gender boundaries. While this made the right hysterical, it made for a bond with voters who shared these formative experiences, which is to say, a large portion of the "ordinary American" population. People liked him when he did things like playing the saxophone on Arsenio Hall's show, and arguably Gennifer Flowers added to his popularity more than she detracted from it.

Nonetheless, Clinton long ago bought into the idea that to win he had to live up to a presidential image that had little to do with who he really was. I suspect that consciously or not, this concern with appearances has had less to do with maintaining public support than with courting the same centrist elite that now resents his failure to slink quietly away. Clinton is a product of lower-middle-class Arkansas who despite his

Yale and Oxford education will never be part of that elite. Instead, in the classic manner of climbers, he internalized both its corporate neoliberal agenda and its demand for moral rectitude. Yet predictably, his efforts to wrap himself in the family-values flag—from denouncing "illegitimacy" and signing the welfare bill to backtracking on gays in the military to the ridiculous firing of Surgeon General Joycelyn Elders for suggesting that masturbation is a legitimate topic of discussion in sex education classes—never for a moment appeased either the right's crazed hostility or the establishment's more subtle disdain.

The essential quality of that disdain was perhaps best articulated by then-*Newsweek* columnist Joe Klein in a 1994 piece on the Paula Jones case. Jones's accusations, he asserts, should be of no interest to the media. They are unprovable, backed by "despicable" enemies of Clinton with dirty motives, and in any case "it can be persuasively argued" that politicians' private lives (John F. Kennedy's, for instance) are irrelevant to their public performance. But, Klein continues, the issue won't go away, because there have been so many "previous allegations of misbehavior" against the president and because "it seems increasingly, and sadly, apparent that the character flaw Bill Clinton's enemies have fixed upon—promiscuity—is a defining characteristic of his *public* life as well." That is, the dictionary definition of "promiscuous," revolving around such concepts as "indiscriminate," "casual," and "irregular," fits the style and substance of Clinton's governing in both good ways (he is empathetic, skilled at bringing people together and finding common ground, able to disarm opponents and forge compromises) and bad (he lacks principle, wants to please everyone, has trouble saying no, fudges the truth, believes he can "seduce, and abandon, at will and without consequences").

In my reading, the not-so-deep structure of this argument

unfolds more or less as follows: Since JFK displayed a suitable, manly decisiveness in public ("acting in a sober, measured — and inspired — manner during the Cuban missile crisis"), we can assume that he was able to contain his sexual weakness, to confine it to the bedroom, where it belonged. His expenditure of bodily fluids did not corrupt, and so the press was right to keep it quiet. With Clinton, in contrast, the media may be forgiven for breaching the proper boundary between public and private, because his own libidinal boundaries appear to be alarmingly porous. He is charming and seductive, wont to "wheedle" and "cajole." "He conveys an impression of complete accessibility, and yet nothing is ever revealed. 'I've had blind dates with women I've known more about than I know about Clinton,' James Carville once complained." In short, Bill is not only too feminine; his femininity is of the unreliable, manipulative, whorish sort. He has let sex invade the core of his being, as we all know women do (this is why it's so much worse for a woman to be "promiscuous"); and it's this erotic spillover, this gender betrayal, that explains (or symbolizes) his moral squishiness in the public realm.

I can't argue with the charge that Clinton is unprincipled; it's exactly this trait that makes him so useful as a trade representative. You would think the corporate elite and their allies in government and media would be more grateful for services rendered. But then, just because you use a whore, it doesn't mean you want to marry her. Clinton put his faith in a protective culture of secrecy that was designed for the JFKs, not for the likes of him — a culture that in any case was dying (though it had protected George Bush and might still have closed ranks around a president deemed to be One of Us). Ironically, despite his "femininity," Clinton also apparently subscribes to a deeply ingrained axiom of masculine conventional wisdom — that the proper response to being caught at infidelity is to deny everything. So he did what reporters would once, in effect, have done for him: he lied. And the combination of a take-no-prisoners right and a spill-the-beans press—not to mention the miracle of DNA testing—did him in.

The Republicans insisted that the issue was not sex, but lies. Right, and what Clinton did was not sex, but whatever. Yet in a way it's true that falsehood was at the center of this crisis—not Bill's third-rate perjury, but the larger lie that he has tried desperately to preserve with his I-am-a-humble-sinner act. The president has behaved like a victim of hostage syndrome, embracing the moral dogma of his persecutors. As a result, although he managed to hang on to his job, he has nonetheless been defeated. For the rest of us, the war goes on.

II

Race and the Ordeal of Liberal Optimism

Optimism — of the will and, if possible, the intellect as well —
is the engine of emancipation. But it is also a tricky business,
often indistinguishable from complacency and sometimes
transparently disingenuous: in America, where it's considered bad manners to defend inequality on principle, proclaiming victory and sending the troops home is an ever
popular dodge. The confusion of an optimism that opens up
possibilities with the kind that merely defends the status quo
encourages (and is in turn encouraged by) a parallel confusion of debilitating pessimism with simple, radical truth-
telling. At a time when a genuine sense of possibility is increasingly hard to come by, debates about social equality tend
to degenerate into shadowboxing between proponents of
"the end of racism" and "the permanence of racism"; between images of "liberated women" who no longer need feminism and abject victims of ubiquitous male violence. Both
stances invite political paralysis, rejecting change as either
unnecessary or impossible.

   As a force in contemporary racial politics, pessimism has
probably been the more destructive, if only because it so often
appears in the guise of antiracist militance. Since 1950, Amer-

ica's racial hierarchy has undergone two successive upheavals: the destruction of the southern caste system and the subversion of whiteness as an unquestioned cultural norm. To claim, as reflexive pessimists do, that these achievements have done little to change racist power relations in this country is to suggest that nearly fifty years of black political and cultural rebellion have served merely to generate new forms of capitulation. This not only insults the people who have engaged in these struggles but endows white racists with an omnipotence that makes further resistance seem futile.

Although the antiracist movements of the past half century have not achieved equality for blacks or "ended race," they have surely opened up possibilities unimaginable before. Black voices are now a loud and insistent part of a public conversation transformed by the expansion of the black middle class and the increasingly multiracial, multicultural texture of American life, by blacks' participation in the media and in electoral politics and their direct and visible impact on mainstream popular culture. To be sure, one effect of the vivid presence of blacks in the public arena is to provide new material for racist fantasy. But a fantasy that talks back is as disruptive as a lover who stops mid-act to complain, "It's not good for *me*." Indeed, the contemporary racial backlash may have more to do with this psychic disruption than with competition for jobs and college admissions.

Yet much of the thinking of the multicultural left depends on the implicit premise that black people are still unrecognized as subjects, that the assertion of black experience and perspectives has left white attitudes, behavior, and institutions unchanged. Of course, it would be foolish to deny that race remains a profound influence on the way most people experience the world and the conclusions they draw from that experience; or that racism is a subtext of much ostensibly high-minded political debate; or that disparities between white and black public opinion reflect racial conflict and alienation. But the question is whether race and racism so completely define us that we are, in the gloomy words of the 1968 Kerner Commission, "two societies, one black, one white — separate and unequal."

A resolve to refute that proposition drives a recent mini-wave of contrarian writings expressing optimism about the American racial prospect. The writers come at the subject of racial inequality from varying political perspectives; but they unite in arguing that blacks and whites share an American identity rooted in the democratic impulse, and that American society is not only capable of transcending racism but is well on its way to doing so — provided the effort is not derailed by defeatist notions of intractable racial conflict. While some of their criticisms are aimed at the right, their target audience is liberal and leftist intellectuals, in particular those who equate optimism with racism and dismiss militant integrationism as an oxymoron. At best, the optimists suggest, this pessimistic orthodoxy inhibits practical political struggle for equality; at worst, it actually reinforces white supremacy.

This latest round of racial polemic caught the public's attention in May 1997, when the nation's two establishment monthly magazines, the *Atlantic* and *Harper's,* ran simultaneous articles by legal theorist Randall Kennedy and journalist Jim Sleeper respectively, invoking the end of race consciousness, not as a utopian dream but as an idea whose time was overdue. In "My Race Problem — and Ours," Kennedy, who had earlier taken up the debate with an attack on critical race theory in the *Harvard Law Review,* boldly rejects the claims of racial kinship. Appropriating Michael Sandel's concept of "the unencumbered self . . . freed from the sanctions of custom and tradition and inherited status," he argues with the communitarian Sandel that this freedom is worth pursuing—and that he as a black American is as entitled to pursue it as anyone else. Solidarity against racial oppression, Kennedy declares, should be based on moral principle, not racial loyalty.

Sleeper's piece, "Toward an End of Blackness," is an excerpt from his book, *Liberal Racism*, published soon thereafter. If Kennedy pins his optimism on the unencumbered self, Sleeper's is anchored to a Whitmanesque vision of America as "a self-conscious social experiment . . . the only multiracial civilization to nourish the seeds of its own transcendence." While Kennedy emphasizes abstract liberal morality as the route to racial equality, Sleeper's primary concern is integrating blacks into a common American "civic culture" whose "genius" is "tempering the universal with the parochial." Untempered, he warns, classical liberalism can end up "soaring into universalisms so removed from human reality that they end up creating holy inquisitions or gulags." Contemporary liberals, in his view, are dangerously disconnected from civil society, "the web of voluntary associations in families, churches, neighborhood groups, and civic, educational, and labor organizations." Directly addressing Kennedy's argument, he points out that Kennedy's self-described "liberal, individualistic, and universalistic ethos" coexists with a personal commitment, rooted in a socially conservative black middle-class upbringing, to a civic culture of hard work, education, and moral responsibility.

In terms of economic issues, both writers are on the liberal left: Kennedy, in a conversation with Sleeper quoted in *Liberal Racism*, defines himself as a social democrat committed to income redistribution, while Sleeper charges that liberals' fixation on racial difference "thwarts a transracial, class politics that could seriously challenge abuses of economic power." Their remarks imply that such a politics could be a suitably universalist way of attacking blacks' economic problems. But Sleeper also links his class critique with cultural conservatism; his idea of how to curb the excesses of the free market includes "denouncing Time-Warner for promoting gangsta rap." Evidently, he would argue that opposing the use of corporate power to pull the plug on forms of popular culture that offend the prevailing civic morality is taking liberal humanism too far. Yet on the subject of racial preferences it is Sleeper, ironically, who is the more adamant universalist, rejecting all forms of institutional "color coding" as racist. In contrast, Kennedy, contributing to a *Commentary* symposium published two months before his *Atlantic* essay, professes ambivalence on the subject. In his view, while affirmative action "has often stigmatized its direct beneficiaries, exacerbated racial resentments," and reinforced "racial and gender selectivity," it has also promoted integration by stepping up the pace of blacks' educational and economic advancement, and has "signaled publicly and visibly a desire to repudiate" the nation's discriminatory past.

Around the same time, historian Stephan Thernstrom and Abigail Thernstrom, a writer and Manhattan Institute fellow, joined the debate with *America in Black and White*. A hefty volume with explicitly Myrdalesque pretensions, *America* aspires to be more than a polemic; it attempts to ground its optimistic claims in statistical evidence and a detailed history of racial progress since the 1940s. Unlike Kennedy and Sleeper, the authors are in no sense allied with the left, and while they explicitly distance themselves from conservatives who argue that racism no longer exists to any significant degree, their book is likely to stand as the authoritative neoconservative text on America's racial condition. It argues that black progress is not primarily the result of the civil rights movement, the antipoverty measures of the '60s, or affirmative action, but was set powerfully in motion by the post–World War II economic boom; and that at present the chief obstacle to continued progress is not white racism but internal problems within the black community, especially the instability of the black family. For the Thernstroms, not only do race-conscious policies, especially racial preferences, fail to address these underlying problems, their divisiveness endangers the advances already achieved.

The other major contributor to this conversation is Orlando Patterson, known for his groundbreaking works on slavery and freedom. His latest book, *The Ordeal of Integration*, is the most eclectic and least predictable of the briefs for racial optimism; its argument elaborates on many of the same themes as Kennedy, Sleeper, and the Thernstroms, while adding his own idiosyncratic observations to the mix. Indeed, if I were asked to choose the work that best embodies the strengths and limitations of the party of optimism, to be placed in a time capsule for the benefit of future '90s scholars, it would be this one. Patterson's great virtue is his determination to resist dogma and to give social complexity its due. Though he can be scathing toward his antagonists—who range from critical race theorists to the cultural right—Patterson often discerns an element of reality in their perceptions. As he sees it, both the condition of "Afro-Americans" (he prefers the term to "African-American" because "Afro-Americans are . . . among the most American of Americans, and the emphasis on their Africanness is both physically inappropriate and culturally misleading") and the current responses to it are "riddled with paradoxes and contradictions."

Overall, Patterson argues, Afro-America is doing better than at any time in the past: economic and cultural integration is progressing, the poverty rate has declined since the '60s from about two-thirds of the Afro-American population to about a quarter, and the problems of the "underclass," while "grim," involve "a small fraction of the urban poor and a nearly insignificant component of all Afro-Americans." Yet it is the growing Afro-American middle class whose rage and despair dominate contemporary discussions of race. In Patterson's view, this is itself evidence of progress: as rigid segregation breaks down, and peace on white supremacist terms can no longer be enforced, painful tensions and conflicts are bound to erupt—hence the "ordeal" of the title. He also notes what he calls "the outrage of liberation" (and others have termed the revolution of rising expectations) in which "a formerly oppressed group's sense of outrage at what has been done to them increases the more equal they become with their former oppressors."

As in his earlier work, Patterson is passionately antideterminist. Attributing the problems of the black poor solely to racism offends his sense of human autonomy as much as attributing them to inferior genes. He argues that "to constantly explain away one's failure as being produced by one's environment, or worse, as the doing of another race or class . . . is to reduce oneself to the level of an object. . . . Determinism logically undermines all attempts to [assert] pride in one's achievements. . . . The cry of the victim, then, is doubly futile: not only does it demean the victim by attributing all agency to the victimizer, but in assuming and legitimizing a wholly determinist social and moral universe, it explains away the injustice of the victimizer." At the same time, Patterson scorns the conservative notion that there is no such thing as society, only individuals: social conditions do limit the scope of individual action, and human beings often act together as collective agents—governments and businesses are obvious examples. In his view, the claim that Afro-Americans must take personal responsibility for their lives in no way invalidates the need for governmental action on their behalf.

Patterson proposes that we stop invoking race as a social category and substitute ethnicity. He would have us speak of "Afro-Americans" and "Euro-Americans" instead of "blacks" and "whites," on the grounds that the latter terms "reinforce and legitimize precisely that biological notion of 'race' that we claim we want to be rid of." He puts the word in quotation marks, to emphasize the artificiality of the concept. Yet he also argues that to try "to solve the problem of 'racial' exclusion by assuming a color-blind world is to assume away the very problem we are trying to solve. . . . 'Racial' categorization is a fact of American life, one that we can do away with only by first acknowledging it." In this vein, he defends affirmative action as the only effective way for Afro-Americans to combat their "isolation from cultural capital and personal networks that are essential for success." In this respect, his own thinking is as paradoxical as his version of the contemporary racial (or "racial") situation. Accordingly, he succeeds in portraying the ordeal of black Americans as far more complex and ambiguous than either conservatives or liberal pessimists allow. In the end, however, he fails to articulate an optimism that clearly distinguishes itself from denial or smugness. Ironically, he shares with both his fellow optimists and the objects of their critique a basic limitation—the inability or refusal to think radically.

Patterson sees "racial" inequality as a purely historical matter, a legacy of the trauma of slavery and legal segregation that takes two main forms: the continuing, if decreasing, isolation of Afro-Americans from the economic and social mainstream, and a serious breakdown of familial and gender relations (which contributes to social isolation and perpetuates poverty). Like James Q. Wilson, he thinks that blacks' economic troubles are best analyzed in terms of class, and he accuses the left of fixating on race as a "means of abandoning issues of class while rhetorically seeming to remain radical." In keeping with his desire to transcode race as ethnicity, Patterson argues that stereotypes of Afro-Americans not attributable to class-linked cultural tensions or theories of genetic racial inferiority should be regarded as "ethnocentric" rather than racist—that is, a function of the ubiquitous human tendency to make disparaging generalizations about groups or individuals who are culturally different, rather than evidence of persistent racial polarization.

But Patterson's premise is wrong: racism is not simply a discrete historical phenomenon or a specific pseudoscientific ideology. At its deepest and most intractable level, it is the displacement onto skin color of powerful wishes and fears about class, sex, and violence—the "dark" underside of a hierarchical and repressive culture. It can hardly be news to Patterson that in the West and its outposts, "whiteness" has signified power, intellectual and moral superiority, and even civilization itself, while "blackness" has represented unreason, anarchic nature, "animal" sexuality and aggression. What he resists acknowledging is that despite the decline of both the racial caste system and the Victorian morality with which it was closely linked, the black-white polarity is still highly charged with psychosocial meaning. While it is no longer intellectually respectable or socially acceptable for whites to proclaim racial mythology as fact (even the genetic determinists invoke it only indirectly, under the cover of dry statistics), unconscious associations live on.

In a backhanded way, Patterson does seem to recognize this problem: in his argument for dropping racial in favor of ethnic terminology, he notes that "black" and "white" are "denotatively loaded in favor of Euro-Americans—as a check in *The Oxford English Dictionary* will attest in lurid detail." The more basic problem, however, is not racial vocabulary but the racist imagination to which it refers. By switching to ethnic designations that are supposed to evoke actual cultural backgrounds and practices (though actually ethnicity too has its mythic element), Patterson means to shift discussion from the imaginary to the real. But since the imaginary in this case has real political effects, eliding it only makes those effects harder to talk about and is, in fact, a form of denial.

The self-definition of black Americans does have an ethnic aspect—there is, obviously, such a thing as Afro-American culture, though I wonder whether blacks with Caribbean roots and those from the American South see themselves as sharing an ethnicity. But the term "Euro-American" makes no sense. To the extent that white Americans identify with their European ancestry, it is with a specific country—Ireland or Italy or Greece—rather than with Europe as a whole; ethnicity defines the differences among whites, not their commonality. For white American Jews, the Euro-American label is even less adequate: Jewishness cuts across racial lines, and those of us whose forebears came (or fled) from Europe regard ourselves as ethnically and culturally Jewish, not Lithuanian or Polish or German; to the Europeans, we were never European in the first place. White people, in short, are in no sense an ethnic community; the only thing I have in common with white Americans as a group is my membership in a majority not marked as different and subordinate because of color. "White" is a purely political category, existing in relation to "colored" and most consequentially to "black." What does that relation signify, at a time when officially sanctioned racial hierarchy is dead?

The argument that conflicts appearing to be about race are really about class ignores the reality that racism has always been a stand-in for and diversion from the class politics Americans like to pretend don't exist. While Patterson is right to charge that many liberals and cultural leftists focus on race to avoid acknowledging class, the remedy is not to deny the intimate connection between the two. It's an old story that poor and working-class whites have avoided confronting their class oppression by identifying with the material and moral advantages of their skin color and projecting their class "inferiority" onto the alien black. Surely it's not a coincidence that the thirty years after World War II—when white Americans enjoyed unprecedented prosperity and security, and muting class tensions was the deliberate policy of government, business, and labor—were also the years in which blacks successfully attacked Jim Crow and white cultural hegemony.

It follows that in the present era of unleashed global capital and "economic restructuring"—that is, open and brutal class warfare—race might once again take on an intensified, rather than a declining, significance. Patterson is correct to note that "the extraordinary growth of income inequality since the mid-seventies . . . is a national rather than a racial issue. *All* middle-class Americans have been losing ground to the wealthiest 1 per cent of families." Nonetheless, the new economic order has generated its own racial "paradoxes and contradictions." Globalism erodes national and cultural boundaries at both the top and the bottom of the class hierarchy, encouraging the formation of a multiracial, multicultural, cosmopolitan elite as well as a multiracial, multicultural, migratory labor force. In the United States, these trends tend to blur the black-white polarity, as the middle class becomes more integrated and non-European immigrants—especially Asians and Latinos—take up more space in our cultural imagination. Yet in response to the same forces, the prerequisites for a genuinely middle-class life—a secure, well-paid job; a pension and medical insurance; a sense of entitlement to material comfort and freedom from chronic worries about making ends meet—are no longer available to most Americans, and are increasingly elusive even for managers and professionals. While upward mobility has mostly become a chimera, the downward kind is all too real. As class divisions widen, the level of anxiety rises among all but the wealthiest whites, and class anxiety arouses racist fantasies no less potent for being unadmitted.

Patterson's naïveté about this dynamic is evident in his analysis of the hostility to affirmative action: he calls the issue a "concocted controversy" because recent Harris polls reveal that only 7 percent of whites claim to have suffered any form of reverse discrimination. While he duly notes and debates the principled opposition to racial preferences (based on the conviction that rights belong to individuals, not groups, and that any official recognition of color reinforces racism), he assumes—rightly, I think—that the popular reaction against affirmative action is fueled mostly by the fear of displacement of meritorious whites by "unqualified" (i.e., inferior) blacks. But he blames right-wing ideologues, "unscrupulous politicians," and irresponsible media for stirring up this fear, rather than recognizing the class panic that drives it.

That same panic propels a fear and hatred of the black poor expressed by an exaggeration of their numbers, the extent to which they are chronically unemployed, and their inclination to criminal or otherwise antisocial behavior. The element of racial phobia in these attitudes is reflected in the fact that growing evidence of a white "underclass" excites no comparable revulsion, while many nervous whites perceive any black stranger, however obviously middle class, as a potential threat to their person and property. Again, Patterson blames these distortions on "an unholy alliance of conservative, law-and-order hardliners, sensationalist media producers, and Afro-American 'race' leaders." But demagogues are only successful when they confirm what a critical mass of people want to believe, which in this case is that blackness and the social depths are one and the same.

For white people, this conflation offers a comforting diversion from frightening truths: that most poor people, black or white, *are* working, but are being paid less than they need to live on; that the basic function of "workfare" is to replace higher-paid workers with welfare recipients and lower the general level of wages; that as productivity rises—largely because of labor-saving technology—the resulting profits go to shareholders, while workers are laid off; and that as "good jobs" disappear, poverty spreads. Middle-class blacks, on the other hand, find themselves in a peculiar bind: not only have they attained middle-class status just when it is less rewarded and more vulnerable than at any time since 1945, but they may at any moment be reduced to symbols of class degradation, subject to insults ranging from frightened glances to the wrath of the police. In such circumstances, rage and a sense of betrayal are hardly surprising.

The symbolism of black and white has also played a central role in the cultural turmoil of the past several decades. The racial nightmares of the day—the unmarried "welfare queen," heedlessly producing children and as heedlessly abusing them; the young male hoodlum who, when not stealing, killing, raping, pimping, or drug dealing, is busily sowing his seed—are lightning rods for the ongoing social and emotional conflicts generated by the '60s challenge to cultural authority and the conservative crackdown. Hatred of "bad blacks" masks secret identification. It represents revolt and backlash in one package: subterranean longings for freedom and erotic pleasure, rebellious anger, fear and guilt, and the compensatory pleasure of moral superiority. Both whites and blacks may perform this psychic sleight of hand, but whites can feel securely distant from their sinister black doppelgängers, while blacks are stigmatized by them. Similarly, pop-cultural styles and images that seek to reclaim bad-black stereotypes as emblems of the rebel and outlaw appeal to young people of both races—but only white kids have the luxury of regarding them as costumes to be enjoyed or removed at will.

This racist psychodrama is a kind of short circuit or hamster treadmill whose main function is to keep people from pursuing subversive questions about cultural norms and values. In the '60s, when mass prosperity intimated the possibility of an end to scarcity, the repressive ideal of work for its own sake came under critical scrutiny; later, as wealth was redistributed upward, that ideal was revived with a vengeance. Patterson uncritically accepts the gospel of work, repeatedly defending Afro-Americans as "hard-working." Yet instead of debating blacks' purported shiftlessness, Americans might more profitably ask whose purposes are served by the current glorification of work—which is to say, of any job, however mindless, deadening, useless, or harmful, that someone will pay a pittance for—as the index of moral and spiritual worth, or by the stigmatizing of the desire for some time of one's own as degeneracy akin to a craving for heroin.

What law of nature decrees that the poor should accept endless work as almost literally its own reward, while the price of hanging on in the dwindling managerial-professional class should be willingness to let one's job consume one's life? Or that any activity that doesn't generate profits (like art and scholarship) or is publicly supported (like child rearing by poor single women) doesn't count as work—and should probably be regarded as a sneaky attempt to avoid the real thing? The logic of the computer age, in which more and more can be produced with fewer and fewer workers, points in exactly the opposite direction: to an economy that can meet people's needs despite a radical reduction in everyone's working hours. But we live by the logic of capitalism, another matter entirely. Not only does the system demand that everyone be willing to work on employers' terms, it's crucial that workers displaced by machines blame themselves—or each other—for being unemployed.

Similarly, the critiques of the family that were part of public discourse in the '60s and '70s are increasingly dismissed (when acknowledged at all) as the irresponsible fantasies of stoned hippies and radical feminist fanatics. It is taboo—

except in the most rarefied precincts of academic cultural theory and, ironically, on the unreconstructed far right—to suggest that the institution of the family and its linchpin, marriage, are in trouble because their basic structure and unconscious sexual dynamics are rooted in a patriarchal system at odds with modernity, democracy, and feminism. Across the political spectrum, the family is regarded as a given, not a social artifact open to criticism but the natural bedrock on which a viable society must stand. (Indeed, the liberal response to conservative invocations of "family values" is to deny that "the family" as an institution exists; there are only various kinds of "families," all deserving of support.) The only debatable issues are how strictly "family" should be defined—should gays be allowed to marry? are single-parent families "broken"?— whether or not the decline of the two-parent family is a crisis, and if so what has caused it: rampant individualism? the demands and values of the marketplace? female employment? male unemployment?.

It is within this impoverished context that the black family has once again become a hot topic. Social conservatives on both the right and the left declare that the Moynihan Report was right, that the high rate of out-of-wedlock births (especially among teenagers) and fatherless households is a, if not the, primary cause of urban black poverty and its social ills. Their opponents respond with stories of strong black families held together against daunting odds by dedicated mothers, grandmothers, and other relatives; or they argue that if there *is* something wrong with black families, it's the result of poverty and social demoralization, not the cause. Rarely does anyone challenge the assumption that "strong families" are essential to social health.

Patterson aligns himself with those (including the far more conservative Thernstroms) who cite the disintegration of the black family as a crippling barrier to integration. He

traces the breakdown to slavery and its "deliberate, ethnoci-
dal destruction of marriage, fatherhood, and the sanctity of
the family as an inviolable social unit," slapping away like
mosquitoes "revisionist historians" who have challenged this
view. Yet as his own statistics suggest and as the Thernstroms
explicitly point out, it is only in the past three decades that a
declining marriage rate and rise in out-of-wedlock births
have made unmarried childbearing among blacks the norm
rather than the exception. In 1960, according to the Thernstroms, two-thirds of black children lived in two-parent families, compared to 91 percent of white children. By 1995, the
number had shrunk to one-third, compared to 76 percent for
whites. In 1960, 22 percent of births to black women were out
of wedlock; in 1994, the figure was 70 percent. Today a majority of black women aged fifteen to forty-five have never been
married, as opposed to 28 percent in 1960.

It would be an unlikely coincidence if such dramatic
changes had nothing to do with the cultural transformations
of this period, especially the sexual revolution and the
women's movement. And indeed, social anxiety about family
breakdown is not focused on blacks alone. Although marriage
rates remain much higher among whites, unmarried childbearing has increased, divorce has become commonplace,
and single-parent families have proliferated. While in the
post-'6os era there is little social pressure to marry or stay
married, feminism and men's resistance to feminism have
generated enormous tensions between the sexes. As women
gain more economic and sexual independence and so have
less need for marriage, they are less inclined to put up with its
remaining inequalities. Men, too, have less incentive to take
on the economic and social responsibilities of marriage and
fatherhood: marriage no longer brings automatic deference,
sexual compliance, or domestic service, while its emotional

demands have, if anything, increased. In response to these centrifugal forces, marriage is flying apart.

But why should these forces affect blacks more? Patterson dismisses as "sociohistorical nonsense" the view that black poverty and unemployment have caused familial instability. He argues that poverty more typically "reinforce[s] the close and intimate bonds of marriage and family, people retreating to them as a haven from the hostile world." Well, yes and no. External hostility does promote communal solidarity, but in urban societies based on wage labor and relative social anonymity, poverty has also tended to weaken the marriage contract: men without jobs or money cannot offer women economic security in return for the privileges of a breadwinner. This effect may be offset in cultures that maintain strong patriarchal norms and marginalize unmarried people, especially women. But American blacks do not belong to such a culture. Indeed, if slavery has contributed to the decline of marriage among blacks, the reason may be less the enforced breakup of slave families than the impact of white supremacy on black gender roles and identities. White male violence against black men attempting to claim male authority — or, for that matter, simple, self-respecting adulthood — has provoked a reactionary strain of black masculine protest. The misogyny that has gone along with this protest has, in turn, occasioned a good deal of female resentment. In addition, black women's exclusion from white cultural definitions of femininity and patriarchal "protections" has made a tradition of black female independence and self-reliance a matter of survival. The stereotype of the black mother addicted to welfare is closely linked to resentment of her perceived autonomy — which is to say her refusal to be dependent on a husband.

From a purely pragmatic standpoint, it's hard to quarrel with the argument that poor blacks must commit themselves to stable family structures if they want to enter the middle class. Patterson and the Thernstroms both note impressive statistical disparities between the economic status of two-parent black families and families headed by single women. But the normative rhetoric with which these statistics are invoked obscures the question of whether it is right that women in a democratic society should be under pressure to marry for economic reasons. It also takes for granted the reason for this pressure—that despite progress toward female equality, the primary responsibility for children still rests on women. Of course, one of the chief functions of marriage has always been economic accumulation, which historically has taken precedence over genuinely "close and intimate bonds," let alone equal ones. But as Patterson, an avowed feminist, must surely agree, one of the great achievements of modernity has been challenging the subordination of personal and sexual happiness—especially for women—to economic and social compulsion.

Patterson is not a nuclear-family fundamentalist; he professes to make no judgment on the nature of familial arrangements, so long as they involve at least two adults and are reasonably stable. But familial stability has always been based on inequality and coercion, and our will to imagine alternative structures of domestic life and child rearing, adapted to the conditions of a free society, has lagged far behind the pace of cultural change. How, for instance, can we ensure children's economic and social support regardless of the relationship between their parents? This society is desperately avoiding such questions. Since the crisis of the family gets to the heart of our sexual and emotional lives, it's even scarier than economic insecurity. The dysfunctional black family, real and imagined, is our image of that fear. The hysteria about the feckless breeding of the black underclass cannot be disentangled from whites' panicky suspicions that their own family lives are, or may soon be, out of control.

At this moment in history, racist attitudes and policies are basically ways of acting out other social tensions. If you disentangle racism from the issues of class and culture that sustain it, there is indeed little left to "race" as a subject of political discussion. Nor can class and cultural conflict be truly understood without reference to unconscious racism: the self is encumbered not only by custom and tradition but by emotions that neither Patterson's rationalism nor Randall Kennedy's liberal morality can adequately comprehend. Patterson's failure to grasp these connections hobbles and ultimately trivializes his argument, resulting in the uncharacteristic superficiality of the book's last chapter, "What Is to Be Done?" The chapter begins with a bombastic paean to the verities: Afro-Americans are "a hard-working, disproportionately God-fearing, law-abiding group of people" who "love and cherish the land of their birth"; as of 1995, "some 67 per cent . . . said that they still believed in the American dream." Patterson then offers a laundry list of goals, ranging from laudable, if vague ("make work pay") to regressive (reduce the number of low-skilled immigrants for ten years and crack down on employment of illegals) to neo-Victorian (fight family breakdown by barring high school boys from participating in sports if they get girls pregnant—apparently the girls have no active role in this process).

Particularly revealing is Patterson's proposal to establish a housing voucher program that will move inner-city residents to the suburbs, "where the remaining good industrial jobs are." Never mind that these jobs, too, are steadily disappearing. What's even more bothersome is that Patterson sees nothing problematic about people having to give up urban life to earn a living, nor does he seem to grasp the irony of his suggestion: suburbanization created the jobless ghetto in the first place. Distaste for the (violent, rebellious, culturally permissive) city and the yearning for suburban safety and homogeneity regularly get displaced onto racial fears and hostilities. But for Patterson, evidently, the suburbs—along with work, family, patriotism, and religion—are simply a mainstay of the American way of life, to which blacks and whites equally (and rightly) aspire. In the course of offering various helpful hints to Euro-Americans on how to improve ethnic relations, Patterson remarks that the "vital source" of Afro-American life is Protestant Christianity, and that "the secular Euro-American suburbanite who wants to understand 'these people' need do no more than recall what she learned in Sunday school." I guess for us secular Euro-Jewish unregenerate urbanites, it's back to the drawing board.

I don't mean to be flip about Patterson's patriotism. His hopes for racial reconciliation, like Jim Sleeper's, are bound up with a romance of America—its struggles to live up to its democratic ideals, its cultural vitality, the centrality of Afro-Americans to both. There is much to be said for this vision; I would describe my own radicalism as stamped with a made-in-USA utopian impulse. But Patterson's call for restricting immigration appeals to a more dubious brand of American nationalism. The problem is not only that such restrictions, however limited or benignly motivated, encourage nativism and undermine the cosmopolitanism that promotes racial integration; or that the more immigrant employment becomes an illegal, underground affair, the more it depresses wages and working conditions for everyone; or even that welcoming skilled immigrants to the exclusion of the unskilled is a pernicious form of class discrimination. It's that the basic assumptions behind protectionism—that there is such a thing as a national economy, which a national government can regulate; that poor people in this country can appeal to the loyalties of a national elite—have been superseded by the globalization of capital.

Patterson is a former socialist disillusioned by his tenure as an adviser to former prime minister Michael Manley's ill-fated experiment in Jamaica. As an alternative to "totalizing ideologies and policies that attempt in any way to micro-manage an economy," he proposes to curb the abuses of the capitalist marketplace through "piecemeal social engineering." But he doesn't seem to realize that it's the transnational corporations, with their awesome power to choose where to invest or withhold their vast economic resources, that dictate economic policy to governments, and not the other way around. While America as an idea, a sensibility, the fount of a popular culture that has become a global lingua franca may still be able to inspire people all over the world, the American government is steadily losing the power to govern in any real sense of the term. Yet the state is still, somehow, supposed to be our collective agent on matters of equality. That affirmative action has become the highest expression of antiracist commitment for so many liberals, black and white, is itself a symptom of a reflexive and misplaced reliance on an increasingly recalcitrant state. Why the fervor on behalf of what Patterson himself calls a "top-down strategy" with inherently limited goals, pioneered by Richard Nixon in a clear effort to co-opt the black middle class and head off demands for more radical—and expensive—measures against inequality?

I agree with Patterson that affirmative action has been a useful tool for combating the subtle forms of discrimination that deprive middle-class blacks of equal access to jobs, education, and "cultural capital." Yet in the absence of a larger social commitment to equality across the board, it has tended to devolve into a statistical exercise that allows corporations and universities to see themselves as progressive and diverse while avoiding lawsuits. The lack of genuine acceptance in this brand of "integration" has become another source of black middle-class alienation. Patterson acknowledges the extent to which affirmative action on campus has led to "ethnic separatism, alternating with periodic outbursts of ethnic, gender, and other chauvinistic hostilities." This development deeply troubles him, as it should. It also seems to surprise him, which it shouldn't. Of course, Jim Sleeper, the Thernstroms, and other racial optimists who oppose affirmative action insist that the very fact of "color-coding" leads inevitably to balkanization. But the more basic issue is not whether affirmative action is a good or bad idea; it's what to do about the gaping political vacuum that affirmative action cannot fill.

Missing from Patterson's book—and others in the neo-optimist vein—is a basic political truth: only a mass movement can produce real change in entrenched social and economic institutions. The racial progress that the optimists invoke is the direct result of the civil rights and black power movements. It is the indirect result of the labor movement and the old left, whose mobilization produced the New Deal and the post–World War II rise in the American standard of living, which created new economic opportunities for blacks, which in turn made the civil rights movement possible. (In one of those fits of amnesia so commonplace these days, the Thernstroms present blacks' economic gains in the '40s and '50s as if the general prosperity on which they depended was a spontaneous occurrence, having nothing to do with the power of labor or the specter of Communism.) Today, the right is organized and the left is not. There is no transnational labor movement to challenge transnational capital, no radical countercultural movement to challenge the repressive symbiosis of racism, capitalism, and social conservatism.

Our situation does not preclude optimism. Experience shows how quickly and unexpectedly political calm can give way to revolt. But revolt is not what Patterson and his fellow

optimists have in mind. In their account, the failure of socialism means that no alternative to capitalism can even be imagined, and they assume that conventional middle-class wisdom is simply real life. In his discussion of the supposed
mismatch between poor inner-city blacks and suburban jobs,
Patterson notes that one possible remedy would be to create
government jobs in the cities, and to give companies incen-
tives to relocate there. But, he admits, "I hold out little hope
for this proposal, given the present mood of the country's
economic and political leaders and the present trends in the
economy." Moving workers to the suburbs is more practical,
he concludes. Patterson's optimism, in other words, does not
include hope for even the most modest of reforms. Optimism
becomes the art of adjusting our ambitions to what our "economic and political leaders" find acceptable. And so, once
again, false cheer succeeds in giving despair a good name.

III

Beyond Good and Evil

I used to dream about burglary. I'd come home and discover, with anguish bordering on despair, that someone had broken down my door and ransacked the place. The symbolism was embarrassingly obvious, but only when I was awake. Over the years I had that dream, I also had a few real break-ins, but none of them were nearly so traumatic — except for the last and, by any rational standard, the least serious.

Actually, it was the second of two burglaries in two successive summers in the early 1980s. The first time, my New York apartment was hit while I was away on vacation; I didn't lose much, and reacted with grumpy urban fatalism. But I must have been more upset than I thought, because the following summer, when I went to spend a month at an artist's colony in a small New England town, I took along all my earrings — none of them worth much except to me — so as not to leave them unattended in the city. At the colony, instead of keeping them in my unlocked bedroom, I secreted them in a drawer in my studio, where I spent most of my time.

A few days later, while I was at breakfast, someone broke into the studio through a window and stole . . . not my type-writer, which was in plain sight, but my bag of earrings. I was devastated out of all proportion to my loss and so enraged at the thief that I truly wished I could kill him in some particularly painful way. *Him:* I envisioned my enemy as vaguely young and raceless, but definitely male, till one day an image of "him" as a teenage girl popped into my head. I was totally disconcerted; there followed a weird moment of what I can only call brain clearing, as my murderous fantasies subsided.

But I didn't really get over the incident for a long time. I got the message, as if it had come from some heavy-handed god out to teach control freaks a lesson; but I couldn't accept it, not with any kind of grace. Still, I don't think I ever had the burglary dream again.

"Crime" — the social issue, the social crisis, the source of recurrent and escalating waves of panic, revulsion, fury, and angst — is not the same thing as crime. When we worry about "crime" we don't mean all illegal activity, or all antisocial behavior. As the left has been so fond of observing (characteristically scoring a debating point while missing the real one), our tacit definition includes "crime in the streets" but not "crime in the suites." Nor does it encompass all forms of violent crime. "Violence" as an issue overlaps with "crime" but is not identical: wife beating, for example, is "violence" but not "crime." Assassinations don't qualify; neither does organized crime, except for car-theft rings and the gang warfare attendant on the drug trade (or more precisely on its prohibition).

The acts that count as crime in the public imagination (I'm dropping the quotation marks, but I mean them to be understood) are those in which the collision of particular criminals with particular victims is unpredictable, uncontrollable, seemingly arbitrary and meaningless. Crime victims go about their normal daily routines and run into the mugger on the corner, the customer who turns out to be a robber, the bullet meant for someone else, the gunman on the Long Island Railroad. They are robbed, raped, killed by intruders in their homes and workplaces, plundered in absentia by burglars and car thieves. The criminals are generally strangers; when they are known—the disgruntled employee, the mother who drowns her children, the kid who opens fire on his class-mates—the act must appear to come out of the blue, to be an irrational, shocking break with ordinary life.

Like everything else, the danger of crime is unequally distributed, a continuum varying from neighborhoods where crime itself is so "normal" that to call it unpredictable or arbitrary is something of a paradox, to those outposts where it remains less a practical reality than an intimation of menace, fed by the media and the knowledge that all borders are permeable—including those that separate housing projects ruled by gangsters from the rest of the world. But what unites the more and less vulnerable is a widespread sense of embattlement against a capricious, malevolent oppressor, along with the worry (or conviction) that government has abdicated what is after all its most elementary excuse for being—ensuring the personal safety of its citizens.

Crime became a national political issue around 1968, and (unlike "violence") it has always been the right's issue, woven into the fabric of the anti-'60s backlash. It would be far too simple to say that fear of crime propelled the right to power. But that fear has been crucial, not only as a potent force in itself but as a focus for more generalized anxieties about social breakdown. While political and social conservatives have explicitly linked crime to the decline of moral absolutism and traditional social authority, the connection is embedded in a cultural psychology far deeper than conscious belief. For the criminal also represents the marauder in ourselves, held barely in check by the institutions and values of "civilization": the family, religion, sexual morality, parental authority, traditional education, the work ethic, unambiguous sexual roles, a clear hierarchy of race and class, a firm social consensus about what constitutes virtue and vice.

These are, of course, precisely the institutions and values that have been radically disrupted by the upheavals of the past thirty years. When politicians from Dan Quayle to Daniel Patrick Moynihan blame crime on single motherhood and call for restoring the stigma of illegitimacy, they invite us to associate criminality with sexual license, safety with self-restraint. Similarly, the right's demand for retribution, especially the death penalty, and its contempt for the rights of the accused speak not only to people's fear and anger, but to their guilt.

The left (broadly defined to include liberals and "progressives" of whatever stripe) has had the same trouble with crime as with social issues generally: committed to reason and optimism, convinced of their moral rectitude, leftists tend to be out of touch with their own messier feelings and therefore with the stew of desire, fear, aggression, and guilt that bubbles in the cultural unconscious. While antiabortionists thundered against baby killing, evoking the specter of moral and sexual anarchy, feminists and other leftists talked antiseptically of "choice" and "reproductive rights" (or, in the case of left pro-lifers, insisted that opposition to abortion is simply about the sanctity of human life and has nothing to do with fear of sex or women). While Ronald Reagan appealed to the longing for freedom and power stirred up by the events of the '60s — effectively linking those desires to capitalist expansion, nationalism, and the assertion of white male muscle — Walter Mondale gamely promised to raise our taxes.

Left thinking about crime has followed a similar pattern. In the '60s, most leftists denied that crime was a real problem, dismissing it as racist code invented by right-wing demagogues. Much effort was devoted to explaining away the disproportionate presence of the poor, minorities, and especially blacks in crime statistics: the statistics were faked; or the police and the courts discriminated against black men, arresting and convicting them more often; and anyway, why harp on crimes committed by the poor and ignore white-collar crime and corruption, not to mention the government's depredations in Vietnam or the legal theft and fraud corporations committed every day? At the same time, paradoxically, many radical leftists proclaimed their identification with criminals as fellow outlaws and rebels: crime, they argued, was a revolutionary act, and all convicts political prisoners. The flip side of this attitude was cop hating; the police represented state repression, brutal by definition. Those who did concede that street criminals victimized people, not least the law-abiding population of their own impoverished neighborhoods, tended to reduce the issue to economics: crime was merely the product of poverty and unemployment, an alternative way of making a living.

I saw things differently. This was partly because my father was a policeman, whose version of the struggle between cops and robbers (not to mention the struggle between cops and liberals) I'd grown up with and generally found convincing, not only because it was firsthand, but because it was informed by far more irony, humor, and respect for complexities than most lefties I knew displayed. Anyway, it was truer by far to the everyday reality of my life in the East Village, where I'd been victimized more than once, where I followed a set of defensive routines (keep the money in my shoe, the keys in my hand during the long walk home from the subway at night; bring the stereo out to my parents in Queens if I'm going away for more than a few days), where I always felt relieved when I saw a cop on the street.

I had no doubt that the cops and the courts discriminated against poor blacks and Latinos; still, the color and class of crime statistics conformed to my experience. As a radical who took for granted that crime was embedded in an oppressive social system, I was not incognizant of my own privilege in relation to the punks I feared. Yet I knew that the core of my fear was not about begrudging a bit of property redistribution. Nor was it only about the threat to my physical person, though that was important; at bottom it had to do with a radical loss of control over the space I occupied in the world. Even before feminism made the implications clear, I knew there was something deeply arrogant about the guys' outlaw fantasies, something I couldn't be part of.

These days, left romanticism about crime has gone the way of left romanticism about a lot of things, and the more blatant forms of denial are rarely heard. Of course, conservatives now dominate the terms of the crime debate so thoroughly that none but the most mildly reformist attitudes get any kind of mainstream forum. But leftists have also been chastened by events. From the '60s through the '80s, inner-city crime — with its proliferation of guns, phenomenal homicide rate, and obliteration of usable public space — rose to catastrophic levels, as black people themselves publicly agonized about crimes committed by young black men. During the same period crime spread out, to middle-class urban areas, to suburbs, even to small towns. Despite the recent publicized reduction in big-city crime rates, caution is now embedded in the social fabric in a way that's inescapable whatever one's political views.

Still, greater realism about crime doesn't necessarily translate into deeper understanding. Bereft of illusions about the innocence of the oppressed, leftists have fallen back on the familiar thesis and antithesis of their ideological tradition: economic determinism (poverty, joblessness, racial inequality, laissez-faire social policies, the fiscal strangulation of cities are the "root causes" of crime) and moral idealism (street criminals are infected with the "me first" greed and ruthlessness of the capitalist ethos or, as the liberal Jewish magazine *Tikkun* put it in an editorial, are suffering from "an epidemic of social alienation induced by the breakdown of community and the triumph of selfishness"). Communitarians and other left cultural conservatives have melded left and right moral arguments, linking crime to rampant individualism and moral relativism in both economic and personal life. While each of these arguments gets at certain truths, in the end they reinforce the most fundamental assumptions of the society they propose to change.

It should hardly need saying that high levels of crime are related to intolerable social conditions, which the left must in any case oppose for their intrinsic harm. Yet criminal acts are not mechanistically, neutrally "caused" by one "force" or another, but committed by people with feelings, motives, and values that shape the social world as well as being shaped by it. Leftists with a moral perspective are well aware of this; they insist on individual as well as social responsibility. But the moral language they invoke poses the opposite problem—it ignores the ways in which our very conception of morality is shaped by culture. By this I mean not how a society supports or discourages particular virtues, but how it arrives at basic categories like good and bad, right and wrong in the first place.

In this culture, "morality" carries the explicit or unspoken modifier "Judeo-Christian," with its profoundly patriarchal connotations. Our vocabulary for discussing values is grounded in the religious equation of morality with God's (the father's) law. We speak of "good" and "evil" as cosmic abstractions, with an existence prior to any concrete act: while evil inheres in our "animal nature" and arises from insatiable material, sexual, and egotistical desires, goodness is Godlike, an aspect of the nonmaterial soul rather than the body, and is defined by altruism, sacrifice, and the conquest of desire. This moral system assumes the need to combat the human inclination toward evil by imposing coercive social controls as well as the internal controls of conscience and guilt. The key institution for its perpetuation is the family: it is parents' job to suppress their children's evil impulses and ensure that they develop the requisite inner controls. Within the patriarchal family, the father is the representation of a transcendent God; through fear of and identification with his authority, children (especially boys) embrace the moral order.

Suppose, though, that this mystical dualism between soul and body is a human invention, designed to ward off terror of unpredictable nature and of our own mortal, vulnerable flesh? That our suspicion of sex in particular and desire in general is part of the same fear? That genuine goodness— empathy, respect for others' rights, a sense of responsibility —does not come from stifling desire but is rather the spontaneous analogue to satisfaction and pleasure in life, to confidence that one's needs will be respected? That evil— pleasure in cruelty, indifference to suffering, solipsistic selfishness— stems not from the indulgence of insatiable desire but from rage at humiliation; not from a swollen ego but from fear that one doesn't exist? This radical, secular view of morality suggests that crime is not so much a failure of the socialization process as one of its logical results; that in demonizing children's desire, the family provokes the very destructive impulses it must then imperfectly repress.

When cultural conservatives, right and left, defend the "intact" family, organized religion, and, in Elizabeth Fox-Genovese's phrase, "some notion, however secularized, of original sin" as bulwarks against crime, they appeal quite overtly to the traditional moral framework. It is perhaps less obvious how that framework applies to the "softer" forms of left moralism expounded in venues like *Tikkun*, which recognize the crucial role of frustration and humiliation in bringing out the worst in people, and indeed make an ethical imperative of addressing psychic pain. Typically, this kind of progressive morality relates individual moral failure to the collective abdication of humane values by the powerful: unjust economic and social policies create both material hardship and intolerable psychic stress that poison personal, familial, and communal relations. Nonetheless, this standpoint implicitly shares the traditional view of morality as the disciplining of desire. Whether posed in individual or collective terms, moral failure is defined as the triumph of selfishness and individualism over an ethic of caring and communal responsibility.

From a cultural radical perspective, in contrast, individual freedom and self-fulfillment are the basis of real morality, and the desire for the pleasures of connection, rather than the subordination of self—that is, a fundamentally erotic rather than altruistic motive—is the basis of a democratic community. The underlying social conflict, in other words, is not selfishness versus caring, or individual versus community, but freedom versus domination.

It's intuitively obvious that happy people don't blow each other's heads off, yet there's enormous resistance to considering that destructiveness may have its source in misery, not some primal sadism. Underlying the resistance is a lurking fear that to understand all is to forgive all, to identify with the criminal and lose heart for revenge. (It's this fear, I suspect, that animates many Jews' insistence that the crimes of the Holocaust are a dark mystery beyond human comprehension, that to try to understand Nazism in psychological or social terms is to trivialize it.) Tracing crime to unhappiness seems to mock the efforts of ordinary people who have bought the idea that their own deepest desires are bad and have spent a lifetime taking pride in repressing them. After all, unhappiness does not *cause* crime, any more than poverty or unemployment does. Feelings of powerlessness and joylessness, rage and despair are common in this society—and not only among the poor—yet most people don't become criminals. If such feelings give rise to destructive impulses, willingness to act on them is curbed—or not—by guilt and fear of punishment or social ostracism.

In this sense, social conservatives are justified in worrying about the relaxation of controls. Thirty years of cultural revolt against social hierarchy, sexual repression, the patriarchal family, and other authoritarian institutions have liberated malign as well as positive energies. Given father's historic role in the transmission of morals, associating crime with the decline of marriage and the two-parent family is not as illogical as it sounds. Yet there remains the basic contradiction in the conservative view: A moral system based on repression and coercion, on the stifling of desire, generates enormous stores of anger and frustration that can never be totally controlled. When those emotions find expression in destructive behavior, it is seized on as proof of intractable human evil and the need to maintain or increase repression. The result is a closed circle, a self-perpetuating, self-reinforcing system of tragic dimensions.

Democratic social movements by their very nature weaken existing authority while intensifying people's consciousness of their discontents and raising their expectations; yet building a democratic culture, laying the social groundwork for a genuine, spontaneous morality, is a long-term proposition. In the meantime, the gap between the decline of old structures and the creation of new ones is filled with all sorts of social disruption. This is our present dilemma, the common theme of our most volatile social issues, from the crisis of the family (women's double shift, the feminization of poverty, children's insecurity, open hostility between the sexes) to the crisis of urban crime. While disruption of any kind makes people anxious and tends to provoke backlash, crime makes the backlash seem necessary, a matter of simple common sense.

Crime is political, although not in the way the left romantics once claimed. Crime is the alternative tyranny, a form of domination inflicted by people who are excluded from the "legitimate" power structure or prefer, for whatever reason, to "freelance." From the perspective of most "respectable" Americans, the established authorities act in more or less predictable fashion—allowing people to avoid punishment by obeying the laws, or by calculating the risk of breaking them—while criminals exercise power arbitrarily, in accordance with their own immediate needs or whims. Since they are not part of any institutional establishment, not answerable to bureaucracy, law, or any tradition of noblesse oblige, they can't be petitioned or bargained with. It's this absence of rules and negotiating room that most terrorizes their victims and makes leftists' comparisons with the "crimes" of the ruling class irrelevant to most people. With minorities and marginal groups, on the other hand, the authorities often feel free to disregard the rules, acting as capriciously as criminals (sometimes actually *becoming* criminals) and exciting comparable hatred.

Crime, like racism, fascism, or authoritarian politics in general, is a means of revenging and redressing humiliation. Since the social contract, as criminals see it, offers them no respect, they command respect with guns. They turn to their own uses the "badness" stamped on their identities by parents and teachers, racism and class bias, contempt for youth, rejection of difference. The most blatant of these uses is masculine protest. The alternative tyranny is almost exclusively a man's world: aggression and physical force are male prerogatives, the streets a male domain. For the iconic black teenage boy in the 'hood and his fellows at the bottom of the social heap, crime can ease the galling contrast between their sense of entitlement to male power and society's merciless erasure. For white men of the working and lower middle classes, who see their status eroding on all fronts, crime can be a last-ditch assertion not only of self but of a social world. Masculinism serves as a bond between the outlaw and his enemies and rivals, the men who yield real social power—which might explain why, though he may savage the real or imagined agents of his impotence (rich people, white people, black people, women, Jews), he more often chooses the targets closest to hand, his neighbors and peers. Revenge becomes another word for self-hatred.

What I'm suggesting is that the psychopolitics of crime are as complex as the dynamics of domination itself. This holds true, I think, not only for criminals but for their victims and for the mass of Americans who clamor that something must be done—or are determined to get hold of guns and do it themselves. Humiliation, powerlessness, violation and negation of self, hunger for revenge are common coin—as is the outrage that one's assumption of the right to dominance (I am a man! I am a white middle-class American!) has been contravened. My point is not that there's a moral equivalence between criminal and victim, but that the issues of power, control, and hierarchy are the air we breathe. The discussion of crime is always about these issues, whether we admit it or not. Crime and punishment, victimization and retribution, repression, explosion, and crackdown are an endless sadomasochistic dance.

Conservatives get credit for being pragmatists about crime, for cutting through blather about "root causes" and demanding that criminals be executed, put away, gotten off our backs NOW! In fact, if this blow-off-steam rhetoric were to be translated into an actual program, it would be more radical than anything the left has proposed. In a society as unruly as ours, hiring more cops, building more prisons, mandating longer sentences are squirt-gun measures. A serious attempt to impose order by force would mean transforming our political culture: requiring a national identity card, which would have to be produced on demand; enforcing curfews; allowing police to stop, search, arrest, beat up, even kill any "suspicious" person and to systematically, openly harass blacks or any group with a high crime rate; permitting forced confessions and imprisonment without trial; restricting defendants' access to legal counsel; restricting the rights of the press to cover criminal cases and police conduct; forbidding groups to congregate without a permit; developing an extensive network of police spies and informers—in short, more or less doing away with the First, Fourth, Fifth, Sixth, Fourteenth, and probably the Eighth Amendments.

There are elements of the hard right that would welcome such a police state, and there's always a danger that people will get desperate enough to support them. Indeed, it could be argued that in an age of no-knock drug raids based on informers' tips and "routine checks" that selectively target black motorists, we are already drifting in this direction. But for most conservatives the point of such incursions on civil liberties, and of get-tough policies in general, is less practical than symbolic. The giveaway is their rejection of the one reform of the criminal justice system that could actually have a major impact on crime. Legalizing drugs would destroy the social basis of an outlaw industry whose entrepreneurs defend their turf and enforce their deals with Uzis; it would end the glut of drug cases strangling the court and prison systems; but it would also contradict the conservative moral agenda. That agenda—restoring the legitimate tyranny of family and church, corporation and state to its historic hegemony—is itself a radical project that would, assuming it were possible at all, take generations to achieve. In this battle to reclaim the culture, fear of crime is a potent weapon. Conservatives *need* crime. Criminals are their rogue cops. Crime gives freedom a bad name.

Since we can't fight crime in a social vacuum, since the comfort offered by tough talk is illusory, we have no choice but to be visionary in one direction or another. We may as well be visionary in the direction of equality and freedom. The hard part is confronting fear, including our own — fear not only of crime but of freedom itself, and the uncertainty that goes with it; fear of our desire, and our violent rage; fear of being the victim and the criminal too; fear, ultimately, of living with our doors unlocked in every sense. Grappling with that fear is the most daunting of tasks. Admitting it is, perhaps, a first small step.

IV

Freedom, Power, and Speech

When the feminist antipornography movement coalesced at the end of the '70s, it merged two debates, one about speech, the other about sex. At the time, feminist opponents of the movement, myself among them, saw the sex debate as our most pressing concern. We opposed censorship as a matter of course, but the arguments against it were obvious, or so we thought, and apparently widely accepted; even some antiporn activists disclaimed any intent to ban pornography, as opposed to raising consciousness about its alleged harm to women.

It was considerably less obvious that many feminists disagreed with the substance of the antipornography argument. The media continually characterized antiporn rhetoric ("Pornography is violence against women," "Pornography is the theory, rape is the practice," and so on) as the "feminist" view; liberal and left organizations that wanted to be seen as profeminist good guys jumped mindlessly on board. Yet the implications of antiporn politics went far beyond what most people took it to be—a simple critique of the sexism in typical pornographic images. In antiporn parlance, "pornography," a word whose meaning had always been slippery at best, lost any semblance of concrete moorings. Applied to all sorts of erotic images from hard core to sexy jeans ads, and said to constitute violence against women regardless of whether it depicted any violence or, for that matter, any women, it became a piece of emotionally laden code meaning "genital sexuality, which is male, which is imposed on women and assaults our sensibilities everywhere we turn."

From that standpoint, which had its roots in a strand of radical feminism dating back to Ti-Grace Atkinson and the female separatists of the late '60s, not only sexual imagery but sex itself was purely an artifact of male power. In her 1989 book, *Toward a Feminist Theory of the State,* Catharine MacKinnon (whose academic respectability soon won her the role of chief antiporn theorist, opposite Andrea Dworkin as chief rabble-rouser) put it this way: "What is called sexuality is the dynamic of control by which male dominance . . . eroticizes and thus defines man and woman, gender identity and sexual pleasure." It followed that female sexual subjectivity and freedom were oxymoronic. (MacKinnon, in an earlier essay: "I think that sexual desire in women, at least in this culture, is socially constructed as that by which we come to want our own self-annihilation.") In essence, this was feminism as a replay of Victorianism: lust is a male vice; all men are rapists at heart; women who want sex are depraved or crazy.

At the same time, antiporn-think was an argument about representation and its relation to the world. The movement claimed that pornographic images (meaning, in practice, just about any sexually explicit or suggestive image) accurately reflected men's view (and only men's view) of women and sex; that these images were a blueprint for and an incitement to male violence; and—the most novel and daring of its propositions—that they were in themselves violent and discriminatory, that is, not simply speech or expression, but action.

In 1984, MacKinnon and Dworkin drafted an ordinance

(versions of which sparked several local battles before the Supreme Court declared the exemplary Indianapolis statute unconstitutional) that defined pornography as sex discrimination. In 1991, the Senate considered the Dworkin-MacKinnon Victims Compensation Act, which, had it passed, would have allowed sex crime victims to sue creators or distributors of sexually oriented material that could be "proved," according to the preponderance of evidence standard for civil cases, to have been a "substantial cause" of the crime (opponents promptly dubbed it the "porn made me do it" or "rapists' liberation" bill). The right, which had always understood the importance of controlling sexual representation, gave these initiatives enthusiastic support: Christian fundamentalists helped pass the "antidiscrimination" ordinances; the Pornography Victims Compensation Act was sponsored by two conservative Republicans.

The feminist opposition has continued to focus on the sexual politics of all these developments—on the reductive (to say the least) view of sex, sexual fantasy, and sexual imagery they imply, the importance for women's sexual autonomy of free access to sexual speech and images (including the freedom to create them), and the ways the antiporn movement has reinforced conservative efforts to pressure women into sexual conformity. But the politics of sexual representation cannot, ultimately, be abstracted from the politics of speech as such; and it turns out that the case against the censors is not so obvious after all. Like the sexual revolution, the expansive definition of free speech that governs current First Amendment law reflects the influence of '60s cultural radicalism; conservative pressures to narrow that definition are part of the anti-'60s backlash. But just as feminist opposition to sexual freedom has complicated and confused the culture wars, so has anti–free speech activism on the left. (For convenience, I use the word "left" to refer to egalitarian social movements, although, as will be clear, I think these movements are divided in ways as profound as the right-left distinction itself—perhaps more so.)

MacKinnon wants both to preserve the special status of sex as a target of regulation and to link it to a more general analysis of speech and equality. In her most recent book, *Only Words*, she makes a convoluted argument: that the line between discriminatory speech and action is fundamentally spurious ("Social inequality is substantially created and enforced . . . through words and images. [It must be] embodied in meanings and expressed in communications"); that some kinds of discriminatory speech ("Whites Only," "Fuck me or you're fired") are commonly understood to be action not protected by the First Amendment; that "speech that is sex," specifically pornography and sexual harassment defined to include sex talk or pictures in the workplace, belongs in this category; that nonsexual verbal defamation of women, blacks, and other subordinate groups is both speech and action; but that in any case, First Amendment rights should not be construed as absolute, but rather ought to be balanced against—or limited by—the Fourteenth Amendment's guarantees of equality. We need, says MacKinnon, "a new model for freedom of expression in which the free speech position no longer supports social dominance. . . . In this new model, principle will be defined in terms of specific experiences, the particularity of history. . . . It will notice who is being hurt and never forget who they are."

It's tempting to be distracted by the author's overheated neo-Victorian prose. Her vivid (hypothetical) scenarios of women being raped and tortured for the pornographer's camera (or killed—MacKinnon invokes "snuff" films as a taken-for-granted fact, though no one has ever produced any evidence that they exist) are of dubious relevance to the First Amendment unless one shares her assumption that photographs of sexual acts involve rape and torture by definition, or her conviction that only under desperate conditions can pornographers "make women do what is in even the pornography that shows no overt violence." On the consumption end:

> It is only pornography, not its ideas as such, that gives men erections that support aggression against women. . . . An erection is nether a thought nor a feeling but a behavior. [Rapists use pornography to select their victims] not because they are persuaded by its ideas . . . but because they are sexually habituated to its kick, a process that is largely unconscious and works as primitive conditioning. . . . It is used as sex. It therefore is sex.

In other words—though MacKinnon never makes the obvious analogy—pornography is a drug that, bypassing will or intellect, triggers male sexual arousal, which is synonymous with aggression ("*It* makes them want to"). Making and distributing pornography is, therefore, no more a question of free speech than "*saying* 'kill' to a trained attack dog."

MacKinnon's obsessive erotophobia gives passages like these a kind of lunatic edge—does she dream, like the authorities in *1984*, of abolishing the orgasm?—that makes her hard to take seriously. Yet the underlying argument about speech and action is not so easily dispelled. This argument was not, of course, invented by feminists or leftists; the boundary between protected speech and harmful conduct is a perennial focus of conflict over the reach of the First Amendment, with conservatives usually on the side of more restriction. (Though MacKinnon brushes aside obscenity laws as obscuring the real issue—women's subordination—the obscenity exception to free speech is based on premises much like hers: that certain words or images unleash uncontrolled lust, which is fundamentally linked to violence and social destruction.) Nor is it likely to be resolved in any definitive way, not only because it's a useful vehicle for hostility to free expression, but because the boundary is not always clear. Saying "kill" to a trained attack dog is one thing, and making porn movies (I would argue) quite another, but what about a telemarketer invading my privacy at dinnertime or spewing messages on fax paper I have to pay for? What if the "speaker" is a computer? And what if it's not trying to sell me something but delivering a political spiel?

MacKinnon is right to insist that "speech acts"—that's why the urge to suppress it arises in the first place. The view of "speech" and "action" as separate domains reflects legal convention, not reality: it makes more sense to think of expression as a particular kind of action, which can be more or less difficult to disentangle or distinguish from other kinds. Ironically, many leftists who want to restrict their opponents' speech on the grounds of its power to wound are the same people who, in plotting their own political strategies, impatiently scorn "all this talking" in favor of "*doing* something." I've often been in the position of having to argue that talking, writing, debating *is* doing something, that, for example, the most potent weapon of second-wave feminism has been speech. But perhaps this is less a contradiction than it seems, for the more expansive efforts to define antiegalitarian speech as actionable discrimination do more than claim that speech is a kind of action, or that the line between protected expression and unprotected action needs to shift: they devalue speech by suggesting that it be regarded as no different from any other kind of action—nothing special, nothing worth risking other goods or subordinating other values to support.

This devaluation is at the heart of MacKinnon's proposal that the claims of the First Amendment be balanced against those of the Fourteenth. "The law of equality and the law of free speech are on a collision course in this country," she bluntly declares. To avert this crash, she would demote free speech from a first principle of near absolute sanctity to one constitutional provision among others, so that laws prohibiting hate speech, for instance, would be judged not only on whether they "trench too far, or not too far, on the right of free speech" but on whether they promote the constitutional mandate of equality.

MacKinnon holds up as a model the Canadian Supreme Court's approach to interpreting the equality and free expression clauses in that country's recently adopted constitution. In the first case to pose a conflict between these two provisions, an anti-Semitic schoolteacher was convicted of violating Canada's law against "hate propaganda" for teaching that the Holocaust had never happened; he challenged the law as an infringement on free speech. The Women's Legal Education and Action Fund (LEAF), in which MacKinnon is involved, intervened in the case, arguing that the law should be upheld in the interest of equality, because "group defamation . . . is not mere expression of opinion but the practice of discrimination in verbal form" and causes damage ranging from "immediate psychic wounding" to genocide. The Court, evidently impressed by this reasoning, ruled in favor of the law. Another case involved a free-speech challenge to Canada's obscenity law, which prohibits "undue exploitation of sex, or sex and violence, cruelty, horror, or crime." LEAF argued that the law promoted women's equality and was therefore constitutional; the Court agreed. MacKinnon concludes, "The striking absence of a U.S. style political speech litany suggests that taking equality seriously precludes it."

The problem with this view is that taking free expression seriously precludes it. What, after all, can be meant by freedom of speech as a political right if it does not include the freedom to debate — or attack — the ideological foundations of the state? Americans are bitterly divided over the meaning and policy implications of the Fourteenth Amendment in particular and the idea of equality in general. We disagree about when inequality is the result of prejudicial discrimination and when it's a legitimate reflection of difference or the fault of the supposed victims, whether inequality is structural or epiphenomenal, and how best to redress such discrimination as we agree exists.

MacKinnon would allow the state to foreclose most of these debates. First, she would dispense with the premise that from a constitutional viewpoint, "there is no such thing as a false idea." Rather, "when equality is recognized as a constitutional value and mandate, the idea that some people are inferior to others on the basis of group membership is authoritatively rejected. . . . Equality is a 'compelling state interest' that can already outweigh First Amendment rights in certain settings. In other words, expressive means of practicing inequality can be prohibited." She assures us, "This does not mean that ideas to the contrary cannot be debated or expressed," then immediately adds, "It should mean, however, that social inferiority cannot be imposed by any means, including expressive ones. Because society is made of language, distinguishing talk about inferiority from verbal imposition of inferiority may be complicated at the edges, but it is clear enough at the center with sexual and racial harassment, pornography, and hate propaganda."

What kinds of policies might follow from this clarity? Well, for instance, "those who wish to keep materials that promote inequality from being imposed on students — such as academic books purporting to document women's biological inferiority to men, or arguing that slavery of Africans should return . . . should not be legally precluded from trying on the grounds that the ideas in them cannot be assumed

false." And, "The current legal distinction between scream-
ing 'go kill that nigger' and advocating the view that African-
Americans should be eliminated from parts of the United
States needs to be seriously reconsidered."

I wonder how MacKinnon would apply her free speech–
equality calculus to the writings of feminists who argue that
banning pornography will not further the equality of women
but will on the contrary impede it. Would she forbid teachers
to "impose" such material on students? Or would it be okay
to disseminate criticism of the antiporn movement, so long
as one did not (as I routinely do with my students) actually assign pornographic images for analysis and class discussion?
Would such assignments be regarded as sexual harassment?
(In the current atmosphere, which has brought us such inci-
dents as a female professor's insistence that a Goya nude be
removed from her classroom wall and a complaint against a
male professor who displayed a desktop photo of his wife in
a bikini, I'd be surprised if this last issue hasn't already come
up somewhere.)

What's "clear enough" from the tone as well as the substance of her polemic is that for MacKinnon, the *principle* of
free speech simply isn't important. Rather, speech is one more
social good the powerless have too little of (she quite rightly
observes, "These days, censorship occurs less through explicit state policy than through official and unofficial privi-
leging of powerful groups and viewpoints"); the powerful and
their allies, too much. Though MacKinnon's rendition of the
clash between free speech and equality is particularly bald (or
bold, depending on your point of view), the broad outlines of
her argument will be familiar to any observer of contemporary identity politics. Its philosophical roots lie in the
Marxist-Leninist-Maoist view of individual liberties under
capitalism as a fiction that masks and thereby perpetuates the
reality of class exploitation. This view filtered into the new left

through formulations like Herbert Marcuse's "repressive tolerance" and into contemporary social movements through its application to black nationalism, the radical feminist concept of sex class, and Michel Foucault's theory of truth as power. Its premise is that domination can be defined solely in terms of power relations between groups, and freedom solely in terms of the ability to exercise power. It follows that any freedom claimed by members of a dominant group is the functional equivalent of an illegitimate exercise of power, which is to say, a form of domination. From this perspective, curbing the speech of the powerful is an act of self-defense.

The antiporn movement, the critical race theorists, black nationalists, some factions of gay activists, and other leftist inheritors of this rationale have developed a variety of tactics for suppressing speech they don't like: advocating new laws, new interpretations or applications of existing laws, campus speech codes and other institutional regulations; pressuring the media, academic institutions, and sponsors of public forums to deny access to certain views and their spokespeople; and if all else fails, shouting down opponents, dismantling their art exhibits, or confiscating their newspapers. These well-publicized efforts have, in turn, inspired the strange spectacle of a born-again civil-libertarian right, charging onto the tracks to rescue the law of speech from the juggernaut of P. C.

I can't fault conservatives for pointing out that the left has driven the "no rights for counterrevolutionaries" train before, with infamous results. Overall, however, their record of commitment to free speech is hardly more convincing than MacKinnon's. They continue to advocate legal restrictions on expression—such as obscenity or flag burning—deemed harmful to morals or patriotism. They are in no way reluctant to put economic and political pressure on the media and the various cultural industries to "voluntarily" censor "harmful" material (or stigmatize it with labels that scare off mainstream distributors). And not only do they accept as entirely right and proper the idea that the press is free (up to a point) for the person who owns one, they are eager to apply this principle to the public sector: just as the owner of a newspaper or TV station has a right to decide which ideas to finance, so the government on behalf of taxpayers should have a right to control the content of pregnancy-related counseling at federally subsidized clinics, federal grants for art and scholarship, public television, books in school libraries, and so on.

In short, the real divide between the "politically correct" and their antagonists on the right is not free speech but equality. Heavily invested in a conception of freedom as a property right, including the right to fight for or maintain dominance in social hierarchies, conservatives have historically viewed any form of government-mandated social equality as tyranny. As the anti-P.C. shock troops see it, the right to engage in what others might call verbal bigotry is not only freedom of speech, but the substance of freedom itself, and so they often cross the line between merely defending its legality and tacitly or openly encouraging it. Predictably, their valid critique of left authoritarianism has segued all too smoothly into a campaign of moral intimidation, backed by considerable money and political power, aimed at demonizing egalitarian ideas, per se, as repressive. They have, in other words, done their best to chill leftists' freedom of expression through the familiar technique of branding their views as beyond the pale of responsible debate, therefore unworthy of access to mainstream public forums and an a priori disqualification for influential government jobs (call it the Lani Guinier Standard).

The truth is that free speech has few real friends these days. Which is to say that while equality is the subject of a genuine national debate (equality for racial minorities, women, and homosexuals, at any rate; class is another story), a ritual endorsement of freedom, coupled with a deeper contempt for it, traverses the political spectrum. It's also true that for all the furor over P. C., in the current political climate the right has infinitely more power than the left to suppress dissident voices. Yet for advocates of a democratic politics and culture, committed to the proposition that freedom and equality, properly understood, are not opposed but symbiotic, it is left assaults on free expression that are, or ought to be, the more alarming.

The right, after all, is just doing what it does, defending established authority. The MacKinnonites—having learned nothing, apparently, from either the devastating history of Communism or the self-destruction of the '60s left—are exploiting the moral clout of equality and justice to attack and discredit the moral value of freedom, and with it the very idea of a libertarian radicalism. This attack does damage not only through its direct influence but through the reaction against it. It arouses in people—particularly energetic young people, the kind that get recruited by enterprises like the *Dartmouth Review*—a host of emotions that feed the racial and sexual backlash: defensiveness about their prejudices, anger at correctnik self-righteousness, the rebellious urge to affirm their sense of self and their liberty by being "bad." It's my hunch that many such people are conservatives (as Trotsky claimed Norman Thomas was a socialist) out of a misunderstanding—namely, that the only alternative to the right is a politics of repression, self-abnegation, and guilt.

While the anti-P.C. campaign continually reinforces this perception, libertarians on the left have not countered it with a publicly visible, *radical* case for free expression. As I've suggested, pro-sex, anticensorship feminists have been preoccupied with showing that the antiporn crusade is about sexual repression, not violence against women, sex discrimination, or hate speech. Though this line of thought suggests one major problem with proscribing antiegalitarian speech—the lack of consensus on how to define same—it doesn't directly confront the idea that free expression as a political value should be subordinate to equality.

There is, of course, no shortage of left-liberal critics of this idea. But too often they seem to think that once they've declared in shocked tones that, why, the proposals of MacKinnon and her ilk *violate the First Amendment,* there's nothing more to be said. Or else they approach the issue as if it were simply a traditional argument about speech-action boundaries, and focus on exposing leftists' censoriousness as inconsistent with their righteous defenses of their own expression: "Free speech for me but not for thee," in Nat Hentoff's phrase.

For the most part, free-speech liberals ignore the fact that "First Amendment absolutism" is a relatively recent development and hardly taken for granted here, let alone in other putative democracies. (Europeans are often befuddled by the concept: I've argued with French Jews who could not be convinced there was no anti-Semitic agenda behind the Supreme Court's decision to let the Nazis march in Skokie; and once, after I'd explained my view of the antiporn movement to a European woman, a human rights activist, she looked puzzled and said, "But free speech doesn't mean you can say *anything* you want!") They have no strategy for confronting the widespread anxiety and ambivalence provoked by the idea that free speech means *anything* can pop out of the mouth of your worst enemy. If anything, some have actively reinforced that anxiety with dogmatic denials that any speech under any circumstances ever crosses the line into threatening, harassing, or nuisance-creating behavior. I think, for instance, of the Brown University student who drunkenly yelled racial epithets under a dorm window late at night, thereby becoming the subject of a major P.C.-First Amendment flap. First the Brown administration overreacted ridiculously; then civil libertarians overreacted in the opposite direction, leading me to wonder what had happened to such useful categories of offense as "disturbing the peace."

Nor are liberal arguments — when the liberals do bother to make them — adequate for refuting MacKinnonism. The standard justifications for free speech take no account of systemic inequality; rather, they presuppose a polity of equal citizens pursuing their visions of truth, expressing their individuality, joining the open debate that constitutes democratic government, competing for influence in the "marketplace of ideas," and so on. Getting closer to the heart of the matter, free-speech proponents have pointed out the contradiction in imagining that the state, accorded greater latitude in regulating expression, would use its enhanced powers in behalf of feminists and other social dissidents rather than against them. (In Canada, predictably enough, the vindicated obscenity law was soon invoked to ban a lesbian-feminist publication.)

Yet even this argument does not meet the MacKinnonites on their own ground, for their implicit claim is that the real political struggle is over who will *ultimately* control government and with it constitutional interpretation. If the goal of this struggle is to establish equality, stripping illegitimate power and privilege from those determined to maintain it, why should powerful, privileged speech be exempt? Why should the oppressed tolerate the enemy's verbal weapons, with their vastly superior delivery systems, while going along with the fiction that speech is a neutral zone? A radical response to such questions — that is, a radical affirmation of free expression as a transcendent political value, not only under conditions of equality but here and now — requires something more than a restatement of ACLU verities: an analysis of the relationship between freedom and power.

The radical left's great strength has been its understanding of power relations. Its disastrous weakness has been its stubborn, phobic avoidance of a project equally necessary to democratic transformation: understanding freedom. To begin with, this means recognizing that power and freedom, however intertwined, are not just different words for the same thing. The mainstream of the left, on the contrary, shares our present culture's thoroughgoing confusion between (to appropriate Orlando Patterson's useful terminology) "personal" and "sovereignal" freedom. Personal freedom can be defined as a particular *kind* of power: the ability to engage in self-motivated, self-generated activity aimed at fulfilling one's needs, unhindered by arbitrary interference or inhibition, limited only by the right of others to do the same. The concept of expression is at the core of freedom in this sense, for such freedom is experienced as the right to be who one is, to reveal oneself—physically, emotionally, intellectually, erotically, aesthetically, spiritually—in action. In contrast, sovereignal freedom is the power to override the limits set by respect for others' freedom, to impose one's own will, to dominate and coerce. From a democratic point of view, it is license.

The blurring of this crucial distinction has its source in the belief—deeply embedded in Western culture, with its dynamic drive toward freedom superimposed on millennia of patriarchal authoritarianism—that the will to power is an ineluctable impulse representing a basic human need, that freedom without the power to dominate is a contradiction in terms. The confusion is particularly acute for Americans, who have embraced the idea of freedom more passionately than any other society. The result is a cultural ambivalence bordering on schizophrenia: the fear of personal freedom as Hobbesian anarchy, and a concomitant acceptance of legal and other forms of coercive social authority as basic to a functioning society, coexisting with the conviction that both personal freedom and certain kinds of sovereignal freedom, particularly in the economic realm, are basic democratic rights. Reflecting this muddle, socialists and communitarians on the left, like free-market libertarians on the right, have tended to conflate individual autonomy with untrammeled social Darwinism.

From my cultural radical perspective, however, the belief in an inherent will to power is a convenient mystification. In reality, the impulse to dominate has its source in overwhelming anxiety—in the fear that not being in control means being controlled, which in a hierarchical culture is hardly unrealistic, and more deeply in the terrifying consciousness of vulnerability to pain, injury, and death that underlies our futile (and therefore continually intensifying) compulsion to control nature. No doubt this anxiety is, on some irreducible level, part of being human animals. Still, if anxiety rather than inborn sadism is the underlying problem of human social life, it's possible to envision a culture that, by recognizing and addressing that problem, will drastically reduce the "need" for power and the reactive need for coercive social controls, greatly improving our prospects for personal freedom (which, for the purposes of this essay, is what I mean by freedom per se).

Equality of social and political power is an obvious condition of such a culture, for a society is free only to the extent that each individual's freedom is respected. And contrary to the communitarian's alarmist image of society reduced to a field of solipsistic, colliding atoms, a radical commitment to freedom requires a good deal of social cooperation: as I've noted elsewhere, putting personal freedom into democratic practice (or achieving what Patterson calls "civic freedom") involves "negotiating social conflicts and deciding on social priorities in ways that maximize freedom and minimize coercion, that allow people the widest possible latitude in meeting their perceived needs while still respecting the rights of others."

By this standard, inequality is an obstacle to freedom not only for the ruled but for the rulers, whose individual autonomy is hedged by myriad pressures, both external and internalized, to keep faith with their group and uphold its class/national/race/gender supremacy. Conversely, real social and political equality is possible only under a regime of freedom. To the extent that any society is based on institutionalized coercion, it sets up classes of coercers and coerced, if not dominant and subordinate social groups, then majorities and dissident minorities, or agents of the state and everyone else.

Yet it doesn't follow that struggles for equality necessarily entail a commitment to freedom. As the depressing history of the twentieth century attests, oppressed people rebelling against domination more typically aspire to take their own turn at ruling, reinstituting indigenous forms of tyranny or inventing new ones. Particularist egalitarian movements, in focusing on the collective power of the group, tend to demand conformity, in the name of unity, from their members, and often fail to challenge—indeed, are likely to uncritically embrace—the ubiquitous patterns of unfreedom enforced by family, church, nation. A movement truly dedicated to expanding freedom must make freedom itself a central question, one that's distinct from equality and worth examining on its own terms.

In this context, freedom of speech, or more broadly, freedom of symbolic expression, can be seen as a radical experiment. It enables us to "try out" freedom, to institutionalize freedom as a social practice, in a limited arena that is at once paradigmatic and unique: paradigmatic in that it is a potent means of revealing oneself in action, influencing the world in accordance with one's needs; unique because it can't pose a *direct* threat to others' freedom—that is, it cannot in itself coerce.

Having made this statement, I'm immediately moved to qualify it. There is such a thing as speech that's tantamount to coercive behavior, most obviously speech that communicates a direct physical threat ("Your money or your life"), discriminatory act ("Whites Only"), or fraud (an ad soliciting mail orders for a product that doesn't exist). Indeed, coercive, as opposed to merely harmful, speech legitimately raises that vexing issue, the speech-conduct boundary; and though adopting this criterion would narrow the disputed zone, it would by no means end debate on exactly where to draw the line.

Besides declining, on the grounds that loud ravings in the middle of the night assault the unwilling listener, to see the aforementioned Brown student as a First Amendment martyr, I would, for instance, argue in opposition to some civil libertarians that following a woman down the street whispering sexual invitations at her is a coercive violation of her space and an implicit threat to her safety and therefore not protected speech. And while I think MacKinnon's equation of sexuality in the workplace with sexual harassment is wrongheaded and dangerous, an invitation to endless repressive absurdities like the bikini-on-the-desk case, I do regard as harassment the deliberate, systematic use of sexual images or speech to ostracize and intimidate a woman seen as an intruder on male turf ("To us, you're not a fellow worker, you're a cunt, so leave or we'll make your life miserable"). On the other hand, unless this kind of harassment is particularly blatant, it can easily be confused with spontaneous expressions of a masculinist sexual culture (pinups, jokes, and so on) that may alienate or offend female coworkers, but are not aimed at punishing them or driving them away. As I said, not an easy line to draw.

Still, invoking coercion as the justification for drawing it does illuminate why freedom of expression deserves special status: not because it is harmless (all controversial speech is harmful from someone's standpoint), certainly not because it is inconsequential (if it were, no one would care), but because, in general, symbolic expression, however forceful, leaves a space between communicator and recipient, a space for contesting, fighting back with one's own words and images, organizing to oppose whatever action the abhorred speech may incite. Though speech may, and often does, *support* the structure of domination, whether by lending aid and comfort to the powerful or frightening and discouraging their targets, in leaving room for opposition it falls short of *enforcing* submission. For this reason, the unrestrained clash of ideas, emotions, visions provides a relatively safe model—one workable even in a society marked by serious imbalances of power—of how to handle social conflict, with its attendant fear, anger, and urges to repress, through argument, persuasion, and negotiation (or at worst grim forbearance) rather than coercion. In the annals of human history, even this modest exercise in freedom is a revolutionary development; for the radical democrat it prefigures the extension of freedom to other areas of social life.

My analysis suggests that freedom is a dynamic social process, a principle of social organization with its own logic—not, as so many on the left would have it, a species of consumer good that can be distributed in proportion to who most needs or deserves it. Nor is it a zero-sum game, in which a gain of freedom for one party automatically means a loss for another, as MacKinnon, among others, claims ("The more the speech of the dominant is protected, the more dominant they become and the less the subordinated are heard from"). On the contrary, both freedom and repression tend to be socially contagious, to expand or contract for the society as a whole. Demands for more freedom, no matter who makes them, upset the cultural status quo and even disrupt the solidarity of dominant groups by tempting their members to value personal freedom over class power; this was at least part of the story of '60s radicalism. Conversely, dominant groups seeking to suppress subversive ideas or acts police their own ranks as well as those of the oppressed.

In any case, the idea of subordinate groups controlling "the speech of the dominant" is at bottom self-contradictory. Such speech is by definition not in danger of suppression. What marks it as literally dominant is its status as conventional wisdom, regarded as self-evident except to eccentrics and extremists: to envision, say, censoring proponents of a balanced federal budget on the grounds that they oppress the poor is too ridiculous even to be good satire. Speech is vulnerable to attack only when its opponents have some measure of collective power and influence, which is to say, the power to silence, and therefore subordinate, the putatively dominant speaker—at least for the moment or in a specific context. During the 1992 presidential campaign, for instance, Pennsylvania's Governor Casey, invited by Nat Hentoff to argue at a *Village Voice*-sponsored forum that liberals ought to oppose abortion, was shouted down by demonstrators on the grounds that his speech oppressed women. Casey was speaking from a dominant position in two senses, as a man and a government official. Yet in terms of the Democratic Party establishment and the liberal community of which he counted himself a member, he was a dissenter, prevented from speaking at his party's convention as well as the *Voice* event.

On the most direct level, a group may use the power of numbers to enforce, through personal pressure, boundaries of acceptable opinion in a particular community or venue. This kind of power, however, rarely has long-term impact unless it is backed up by genuinely powerful institutions—government agencies, universities, media corporations—with an interest in stifling speech so crudely "dominant" as to disrupt business as usual or contradict their official claims of tolerance and enlightenment. It is, after all, the people who run things who have the most to lose when offensive, provocative words rock the boat.

Consider the infamous Andy Rooney affair. The *60 Minutes* commentator was attacked by the Gay and Lesbian Association against Defamation (GLAAD) for publishing a crude, antigay letter in the gay newspaper the *Advocate* and allegedly making racist remarks to a reporter. As a result he was suspended from CBS, and elicited reproving editorial noises about "civil public discourse" from the *New York Times*. This was seen in some quarters as a victory for the left. Yet the real reason Rooney got into trouble was that he violated the media establishment's bland, centrist criteria for acceptable speech. In demanding Rooney's removal, lesbian and gay activists appealed to precisely those standards of "civility"—that is, niceness—regularly used to marginalize their own speech. While Rooney was slapped down for expressing bluntly illiberal views, it's hard to imagine anyone comparably left of the mainstream—particularly in a libertarian direction—ever having his job in the first place. And suppose such a person did slip through and then wrote a letter to the editor defending illegal drug use or attacking organized religion as tyrannical—can anyone doubt that he or she would have been not suspended but fired, and with little public protest at that?

The expression of a homophobic opinion is not an act of domination. Where the real issue of inequality arises is in the consistent denial to cultural radical dissidents of equal access to the mass media and other public forums. Rather than pressuring CBS to throw Andy Rooney off the air, GLAAD should have demanded time on *60 Minutes* to rebut him. In choosing instead to define his speech as an intolerable threat, they merely reinforced the basic assumption of the dominant culture that we can't afford freedom, that all hell will break loose if we relax controls. In effect, campaigns against offensive speech displace the fight for equality onto battles against freedom. This is a tempting maneuver, particularly at a time when the left is weak and on the defensive, for a simple reason: fighting for equality is a difficult, long-term, exhausting process that meets bitter resistance every step of the way, while attacks on freedom often get immediate results and — odd, isn't it? — sympathy or even outright support from the very people in power who are supposed to be the enemy.

Efforts to restrict the "speech of the dominant" are also an intellectual preemptive strike: they proceed from the assumption that the nature of inequality is a settled issue, that the left's understanding of unequal power relations as systemic and pervasive is self-evidently valid. In fact, while this conception of power has had considerable impact on American racial and sexual politics, it remains highly controversial — disputed not only by most members of dominant groups, but by a good many of the blacks, women, and others it defines as oppressed. Categorically defining pornography as an instrument of systemic inequality is even more problematic, given the passionate disagreement of so many militant feminists. When movement activists pressure the state or other institutions to enforce such views, they short-circuit the democratic process of persuasion even among their own supposed constituencies, those very groups whose equality is at stake. Instead, they characteristically dismiss the inconvenient fact of disagreement among the oppressed as a kind of invasion of the body snatchers — dissenters are whites in blackface, male-identified women, and so on.

Invariably, such labels get applied to an ever widening range of targets, from out-and-out conservatives (the Phyllis Schlaflys and Clarence Thomases) to those who merely differ with the movement or its self-appointed representatives on some item of prevailing opinion. Often it is dissenting radicals who are subject to the most vicious attacks: the antiporn movement accuses its feminist opponents of celebrating patriarchy and violence against women; black feminists are vilified as allies of the white power structure for criticizing sexism among blacks. It's impossible, in short, to censor the speech of the dominant without stifling debate among all social groups and reinforcing orthodoxy within left movements. Under such conditions a movement can neither integrate new ideas nor build support based on genuine transformations of consciousness rather than guilt or fear of ostracism. Again the casualty is freedom, both as process and as aim. Power becomes all that matters.

The radical social movements that came out of the '6os left have shared a fundamental belief—that inequality is not simply a legal matter, that it pervades the institutions and practices of social, economic, and cultural life, that "the personal is political." They have specifically and repeatedly rejected the liberal emphasis on law and government as the primary locus of political power. MacKinnon and other social-movement activists who oppose free speech regard themselves as the standard bearers of this radical tradition. As they see it, those of us who call ourselves libertarian or democratic radicals are (at best) merely liberals who, in claiming that oppressed groups benefit from an expansive reading of the First Amendment, ignore the imbalance of social power under the legal facade. Thus MacKinnon, in a 1986 essay on sexual politics and speech: "The First Amendment was conceived by white men from the point of view of their social position. Some of them owned slaves; most of them owned women. . . . They wrote [it] so their speech would not be threatened by this powerful instrument they were creating, the federal government. . . . Those whose speech was silenced prior to law . . . were not secured freedom of speech."

In the context of this argument, it's ironic — on the surface, at least — that self-proclaimed radicals should put so much importance on harnessing the power of the state to control speech. If inequality is embedded in every facet of the culture, if the antidiscrimination laws (and constitutional interpretations) that already exist have done relatively little to disrupt these tenacious social patterns, what would be accomplished by adding anti–discriminatory speech laws and court rulings? Such measures would no doubt increase the already conspicuous gap between what people think and what they dare to say, forcing them to develop ever more elaborate codes to circumvent the censors. And for the time being (until the new codes began, inevitably, to carry the same charge as the words they replaced), vulnerable groups would get some relief from the unquestionably painful, alienating experience of hearing explicit contempt and hostility spewed in their direction. But the prospect of more genteel hypocrisy smoothing over the ragged edges of power is hardly a radical cause.

MacKinnon's view of the state embodies another superficially puzzling contradiction. The First Amendment was written by (white) men to codify their relations with the state and was not meant to apply to women, whose speech was silenced by male social power. Therefore, MacKinnon contends, women have no stake in, and no use for, First Amendment rights — on the contrary, men use them against us. The Fourteenth Amendment, on the other hand, was also written by men, who had explicitly rejected the idea of extending the franchise to women along with black men, and certainly did not mean "equal protection of the laws" to include social and cultural equality. Yet MacKinnon doesn't doubt that feminists can use it in women's behalf.

In writing about speech, she simply ignores the fact that women have long since won the battle to become actors (however unequal) in the public sphere, and have expanded the meaning of the First Amendment by challenging the suppression of birth control information, material on female sexuality, feminist polemics, and other forms of "obscenity." In writing about equality, she not only assumes that feminists and other leftists can fight to expand the meaning of the Fourteenth Amendment, but that they can fight successfully, the continuing political, social, and cultural domination of white men — and the "silencing" of women and minorities — notwithstanding. This is, of course, an untenable attempt to have it both ways: either the state at any given moment reflects, at least to some extent, the social and cultural conflicts of the society as a whole, and fighting to expand both First and Fourteenth Amendment rights can be part of a larger struggle for freedom and equality, or else the state is the monolithic instrument of a white male ruling class, in which case the only honorable course is an uncompromising attack on its authority.

But MacKinnon's position makes emotional if not logical sense. Because she equates freedom with coercive power, it follows that because men (for instance) subordinate women and not vice versa, men's freedom is merely the liberty to do their brutal worst, while women's freedom has no concrete existence, and can be realized in the imagination only as the power to curb the freedom (that is, the sadism) of men. (This inability to see women as exercising even limited autonomy leads to the sort of cognitive dissonance whereby MacKinnon can declare women to be definitively silenced, even as she herself is an outspoken and influential public figure.) Nor does her indictment of the liberal state as an instrument of men's collective power translate into any genuinely felt fear of extending its control. Rather, in the long tradition of Hobbesianism on both the left and the right, MacKinnon implicitly regards the state, and specifically the law (she is, after all, a lawyer), as a check on the will to power. In her cultural unconscious, the law is superego to men's terrifying id, and therefore the ideal vehicle for women's resistance to victimization.

For all practical purposes, MacKinnonism signals retreat from a radical democratic politics of cultural transformation—which requires constant discussion and debate, openness to new ideas, respect for people's expressed needs and desires, tolerance of uncertainty and complexity—to the old-time left religion of seizing the state in the name of the oppressed and imposing equality, as the seizers define it, from the top. This seems, for a significant portion of the broadly defined left, to be the dream that will not die, despite the nightmare it turned out to be in real life. The persistence of the statist model and what it represents—fear of the will to power congealed into the very thing it fears—is arguably the biggest obstacle to real radicalism.

Some years ago, at a feminist conference in what was then Yugoslavia, I was struck by the fierce scorn of the Eastern European participants for utopian language of any sort. The Americans were firmly informed that certain words had been so discredited by the Communists' use of them that they were literally unspeakable—words like "emancipation," "liberation," "revolution," even "organize" and "struggle." The burden of proof is on those of us who seek to reclaim such words. To be credible, that quest requires a decisive break with the logic of countervailing power, whereby movements get trapped in a cycle of rebellion and repression and the culture continues to chase its own tail, in favor of a logic of freedom that follows the contours—convoluted to be sure, but also open-ended—of human possibility. Which is to say that the debate over speech, like the debate over sex, reflects irreconcilable visions of the good life and the good society, calling into question the very definition of the left or even (speaking of reclaiming words) whether "left" as a category of social aspiration has any clear meaning at all.

It makes sense that feminism should be at the vortex of this conflict. At its core, feminism is about freedom: seeking women's self-determination in private as well as public life; asserting women's individual human subjecthood against the pervasive social understanding of woman as a natural resource that exists for the benefit of men and children. Radical feminists, asking what impeded that freedom, developed an analysis of men's collective power over women. As the critique of male power is increasingly unmoored from a commitment to women's freedom—and used instead to "protect," that is, control us—it is easy to forget that these concerns once merged to create the most dynamic cultural radical movement in modern history. In one generation, feminism irreversibly shattered the culture's common sense about sex and gender. We called that process consciousness-raising. What we meant, first of all, was that we had found our voices, seized our freedom—and our power—of speech.

V

Intellectual Work in
the Culture of Austerity

On the crudest level, the lives of American intellectuals and artists are defined by one basic problem: how to reconcile intellectual or creative autonomy with making a living. They must either get someone to support their work—whether by selling it on the open market or by getting the backing of some public or private institution—or find something to do that somebody is willing to pay for that will still leave them time to do their "real work." How hard it is to accomplish this at any given time, and what kinds of opportunities are available, not only affect the individual person struggling for a workable life, but the state of the culture itself. This tension between intellectual work and economic survival is thoroughly mundane and generally taken for granted by those who negotiate it every day; but to look at the history of the past thirty years or so is to be struck by the degree to which the social, cultural, and political trajectory of American life is bound up with this most ordinary of conflicts. During that time, the conditions of intellectual work have radically changed, as a culture operating on the assumption of continuing—indeed increasing—abundance has given way to a culture of austerity.

In the 1960s, prosperity and cultural radicalism were symbiotic: easy access to money and other resources fueled social and cultural experimentation, while an ethos that valued freedom and pleasure encouraged people's sense of entitlement to all sorts of goods, economic and political. For many of us, the "excess" of the '60s meant the expansion of desire and fantasy, but also (and not coincidentally) of money and time. I (a child of the hard-working lower middle class) found it relatively easy to subsist as a freelance writer in New York. With a fifty-dollar-a-month rent-regulated East Village apartment, I could write one lucrative article for a mainstream magazine and support myself for weeks or even months while I did what I liked, whether that meant writing for countercultural publications that couldn't pay or going to political meetings. When I did have jobs, I didn't worry overmuch about losing them, and so felt no impulse, let alone need, to kiss anyone's ass. There was always another job, or another assignment. At one point, while I was living with a group of people in Colorado, the money I made writing (sporadically) about rock for the *New Yorker* was supporting my entire household.

Throughout this period, cheap housing was the cement of cultural communities. It allowed writers and artists to live near each other, hang out together. It invited the proliferation of the underground press and alternative institutions like New York's Free University, with its huge loft off Union Square, where just about all the leftists and bohemians in town congregated at one time or another. Prosperity also financed travel, and with it the movement of ideas; encouraged young people to avoid "settling down" to either careers or marriage; and even made psychotherapy, with its ethos of autonomy and fulfillment, a middle-class rite of passage subsidized by medical insurance. This climate of freedom in turn fomented dissident politics—which, contrary to much recent and dubious rewriting of history, included class politics. Although the distinctive quality of the '60s social movements, from ecology to feminism, was their focus on the kinds of concerns that surface once survival is no longer in question, economic issues were by no means ignored. Criticism of capitalism and economic inequality was part of mainstream public debate. There was significant liberal pressure to extend the welfare state, while at the same time the new left was challenging "corporate liberalism" and its social programs as fundamentally conservative, a way of managing inequality rather than redressing it.

Since the early '70s, however, the symbiosis has been working in reverse: a steady decline in Americans' standard of living has fed political and cultural conservatism, and vice versa. Just as the widespread affluence of the post–World War II era was the product of deliberate social policy—an alliance of business, labor, and government aimed at stabilizing the economy and building a solid, patriotic middle class as a bulwark against Soviet Communism and domestic radicalism—the waning of affluence has reflected the resolve of capital to break away from this constraining alliance. In 1973, as the United States was losing both the Vietnam War and our position of unquestioned economic dominance in the world, the formation of OPEC and the resulting "energy crisis" signaled the coming of a new economic order in which getting Americans to accept less would be a priority of the emerging multinational corporate and financial elite. By then the reaction against the culture and politics of the '60s was already in progress. With the end of cheap, freely flowing gasoline—the quintessential emblem of American prosperity, mobility, and power—the supposed need for austerity began to rival law and order as a central conservative theme.

For the cultural right, austerity was not just an economic but a moral imperative; not mere recognition of what was presented as ineluctable necessity but a new weapon against the "self-indulgence" and "hedonism" that had flowered as masses of Americans enjoyed a secure and prosperous existence. For the economic elite, whose objective was convincing the middle class that the money simply wasn't there, whether for high wages or for social benefits, this brand of moralism served a practical function: in diverting people's attention from the corporate agenda to their own alleged lack of social discipline and unrealistic expectations, it discouraged rebellion in favor of guilty, resigned acquiescence.

The determination of corporate capital to enforce a regime of austerity provoked a pivotal event: the New York City fiscal crisis of 1975. New York was not only the chief national center of intellectual and cultural activity but the proud standard bearer of a political ethos that reflected its history as a center of working-class activism. New Yorkers maintained a militant sense of entitlement to a high level of public services and social supports—including a free college education—unequaled anywhere else in the country. When the banks pulled the plug on the city's credit, this was not simply a financial decision—indeed, more than one analysis of the situation has concluded that it was unnecessary from a purely economic point of view (see, for example, Jack Newfield and Paul Du Brul, *The Abuse of Power: The Permanent Government and the Fall of New York* [Viking Press, 1977], or Eric Lichten, *Class, Power, and Austerity: The New York City Fiscal Crisis* [Bergin and Garvey, 1986]). It was a political act motivated by the will to destroy New York's pro-worker, anticorporate political culture, with its immense symbolic importance as a flagship of resistance: if austerity could be imposed on New York, it could be imposed anywhere. In essence, the specter of bankruptcy was a pretext for breaking the power of the municipal unions and forcing the city to shrink its public sector, while successfully convincing the population that there was no point in taking to the streets. To this end, economic restrictions were coupled with a relentless moral attack on the city, particularly the supposedly greedy city workers who had gotten us into this mess. New Yorkers (so the next few years' worth of clichés would have it) had been selfish profligates living beyond their means, but now the days of wine and roses were over, and we would have to shape up, lower our expectations, tighten our belts.

The rhetoric of austerity, embraced by the Carter administration, quickly spread from New York to the rest of the country. By 1980 it appeared that Americans had had enough; rejecting the ascetic Jimmy "Moral Malaise" Carter, they opted for Ronald Reagan's vision of limitless opportunity and his up the rich, damn the deficit guns-and-tax-cuts policy. Yet paradoxically, it was in the so-called decade of greed that the culture of austerity became solidly entrenched. As public services and amenities were increasingly deemed an unconscionable extravagance, the very idea of a public life whose rules and values rightly differed from those of the private market came into disrepute. As personal morality was conflated with productivity and adherence to the work ethic, business was held to be the model for how all organizations, regardless of their purpose, ought to operate: tightly controlled from the top, obsessed with the bottom line, and "efficient," that is, uninhibited by sentimentality about the welfare of their workers or the surrounding community. Most ominously for the future of democracy, it came to be taken for granted that basic decisions about public spending, taxes, regulation, and economic policy generally would be made, not by our elected representatives, but by corporations prepared to withhold credit or move their capital and jobs elsewhere in response to any government foolish enough to defy their disapproval. Today all these propositions are virtually unquestioned axioms of economic, political, and cultural common sense.

The culture of austerity has had a profoundly depressing

effect on intellectual life. Most obviously, its axioms reinforce and rationalize an actual material scarcity. It is harder and harder to find support for any sort of intellectual or creative work that can't be mass-marketed or subsidized by corporate-financed conservative foundations and think tanks: public funds for scholarship and the arts are drying up, book publishing and journalism are dominated by conglomerates, full-time faculty jobs are giving way to academic piecework at poverty-level wages. People work longer and more exhausting hours, often at more than one job, just to get by; they have little time, energy, or money with which to launch alternative publications, schools, and other cultural experiments. In New York and other major cultural centers, real estate inflation, spurred by tax giveaways to developers, disinvestment in public housing and creeping deregulation (New York's co-op conversion movement, which went into high gear in the '80s, was essentially a scheme for property owners to "liberate" rent-stabilized apartments to be sold and in many cases re-rented at market rates) has led to prohibitive rents that chase writers, artists, and students out of convenient downtown neighborhoods while ensuring that discretionary income is an oxymoron. Nor can groups afford to rent large, easily accessible spaces for cultural and educational activities. (Under present conditions, the Free University would have to be on Staten Island.)

Austerity has also reinforced the characteristic anti-intellectualism of American culture, deeply rooted in a combination of business-oriented and populist attitudes, which takes thinking, imagining, and learning with no immediate instrumental object to be a useless luxury rather than work in any meaningful sense. After all, such activities are not quantifiable in terms of how much they add to the GDP, nor are they easily rationalized in terms of working hours. Furthermore, they are pleasurable; therefore it seems unfair that they should be economically rewarded. In fact, they are regarded not only as pleasure but as infantile narcissistic gratification, as one might infer from such locutions as "They're off contemplating their navels," or "thumbsucker" as a pejorative term for essay. Intellectual occupations excite suspicion because they are always at least potentially outside social control; at the same time, they are perceived and widely resented as a source of power and influence and as the preserve of an elite that is getting away with not putting its nose to the grindstone.

In the service of this *ressentiment*, it is the current fashion to insist that intellectual enterprises like publishing and education prove their mettle in the marketplace by embracing corporate goals, management techniques, and standards of cost effectiveness. The huge media companies that control trade publishing will not tolerate the traditionally low profits on so-called mid-list books, let alone subsidize worthy money-losers as the old independent houses did. At the same time, universities are reducing or eliminating subsidies to their own presses, whose decisions about publishing books and keeping them in print are increasingly dictated by market considerations. University presidents at both public and private institutions adopt the language of CEOs charged with reducing labor costs, increasing "productivity" (i.e., faculty workloads and class sizes), cutting and consolidating programs in the name of efficiency, and becoming more "accountable" to their "customers" (variously construed as the taxpayers who fund them, the employers that hire their graduates, or the parents who pay tuition—rarely the students themselves). Increasingly, they demand that faculty become entrepreneurs, raising outside money to support their programs.

Tax law and IRS policy reflect the same mentality. Writers and artists, who may have to live for years on an advance or the income from one major commission, are no longer permitted to average their incomes over several years for tax purposes, and the rules for deducting the cost of a home office are so strict few freelancers working in small apartments can qualify. The policy that allowed publishers to deduct the costs of warehousing their unsold inventory was rescinded on the grounds that a book is no different from any other product, a move that in effect penalizes companies for keeping slow-moving books in print. As a result, thousands of books that might have sold a few copies a year are remaindered or shredded. Postal subsidies for books and periodicals have been abolished. Shrinking the space for independent intellectual and cultural activity is no mere unfortunate byproduct of such exercises in corporatethink but their fundamental logic and purpose.

For some time my own working life was relatively insulated from the culture of austerity. During the '70s, I was a columnist or contributing editor at various magazines and in 1979 began working as a staff writer at the *Village Voice*, which had become a highly successful commercial enterprise while remaining, in crucial respects, a countercultural institution. Rupert Murdoch had bought the *Voice* two years earlier, much to the consternation of the staff, which promptly unionized. But after a few initial skirmishes — his first act was to fire the editor; a staff walkout forced him to back down — he had made no serious moves (at least in public) to change the paper's content or its freewheeling culture. By the time I joined the staff, he had managed to install his own appointee, David Schneiderman, as editor-in-chief. But Schneiderman (who hired me) proved to be a staunch defender of the *Voice*'s independence, staving off his boss's persistent complaints about the paper and demands to fire writers whose politics offended him or whose investigative zeal impinged on his and his friends' interests. Schneiderman was able to get away with this because the *Voice* was making huge profits at a time when Murdoch was financially stretched by his efforts to build his media empire.

In contrast to the hierarchical system typical of magazines and newspapers, the structure of authority at the *Voice* was loose and decentralized. Editing was a collaborative process in which a writer and an editor came to an agreement on the final version of a piece; the editor-in-chief might make objections or suggestions, but only in the rarest of cases were the writer or original editor overruled. Both writers and editors were militantly protective of their autonomy and notoriously contentious. Having come of age during the economic boom and cultural revolt, we still had a '6os sense of entitlement, were neither afraid of nor reverent toward authority, and believed that we who gave the paper its character were really its rightful owners. (This sentiment was not shared by the noneditorial employees, who were much more regimented.) Furthermore, the *Voice*'s identity as a "writer's paper" and its claim on the loyalty of its audience depended on its stable of writers, who knew they couldn't easily be replaced. As a result, management's sporadic and tentative attempts to rationalize the paper and bring the staff under more control met stiff resistance and were, in literal bottom-line terms, more trouble than they were worth. The trade-off was that we were paid much less than journalists in comparable positions at other publications (if no longer the ridiculous pittance of the underground-paper, pre-union days), a major reason the *Voice* was so profitable.

And so, through the first years of the Reagan era I still led a freelancer's life, controlling my own time. My income was small but adequate given my rent, which had gone up quite a bit since the '6os, but owing to rent stabilization was still pretty cheap. The *Voice* office, where I hung out a lot, was a short walk from my apartment (in the West Village now), and most of my friends lived nearby. I belonged to a lively community of journalists and to a feminist group; in these circles the ethos of sex, dope, and rock and roll was by no means passé. Though I felt the sting of the cultural backlash and worried, rather abstractly, about my economic future, my day-to-day habits were unaffected.

Then I met a man I wanted to live with and had a baby. Many changes ensued, not least my induction into the new economic order. My apartment was too small for three, and in Reagan's morning-in-America rental market, finding an affordable (i.e., rent-regulated) alternative in the neighborhood required both ace detective skills and large bribes. So we moved away from the Village and eventually bought a co-op in Brooklyn, forty-five minutes by subway from my old haunts and four times as expensive, in terms of monthly carrying costs, as my old rent. (As for its value as an investment, that collapsed with the stock market in 1987.) Since I needed more money—as well as some concrete reason to be in Manhattan regularly so as not to get totally sucked into domestic life—I asked the *Voice* for an editing job. I would only work part-time, though, and not simply because I wanted to spend time with my daughter; for me it was a matter of principle not to sign on to a forty-hour week unless I had no choice. I hadn't had a full-time job in fifteen years. My personal solution to the tension between earning a living and preserving my autonomy was institutional marginality. While I hadn't rejected institutions altogether, as many '6os bohemians had done, I liked to keep my distance.

This was not an issue at the *Voice*, where writers and editors had all sorts of idiosyncratic arrangements. So long as you did your work, no one much cared when you did it or where or on what terms. In fact we worked very hard—I certainly put in many more hours than I'd officially agreed to—

but we were driven by passion and perfectionism, not subordination. Even as an editor, I preserved as much as I could of my freelance mentality: one summer, wanting to leave town, I estimated the extra hours I'd worked so far that year and announced that to make up the time I was taking an extra month's vacation. My boss, the editor-in-chief (a successor to Schneiderman, who had been promoted to publisher), acceded to my plan, albeit without great enthusiasm. For me, this kind of freedom was worth any amount of the money I might have made at an uptown magazine.

When birdseed tycoon Leonard Stern bought the *Voice* in the mid-'80s, it was clear that he and Schneiderman were impatient with an editorial culture that, from the viewpoint of conventional business practice, bordered on anarchy. To be fair, their perception of an impossibly unruly staff was not wholly unjustified. Freedom of expression at the paper was often indistinguishable from egomania and bullying, as certain writers were in the habit of throwing tantrums—at editorial decisions they disagreed with, editors' suggesting that their deathless words might be a tad fewer in number, or underlings' insufficient servility. The long-running culture war at the *Voice*—the old guard of straight male lefty politicos and "hard" newswriters (dubbed "the white boys" by their antagonists) versus the "thumbsucking" critics and essay writers, many of them feminist and gay activists (though only marginally less white)—kept erupting into vicious public fights. Trying to run a railroad in the midst of this constant fractiousness was no enviable task. And as the culture of austerity tightened its grip, the effort must have begun to seem not only anomalous but an exercise in antediluvian masochism.

Since moving to the business side of the paper, Schneiderman had hired two editors-in-chief, neither of whom had taken charge the way he'd hoped. In 1988 he settled on a third, who, unlike his ill-fated predecessors, was utterly disdainful of the *Voice*'s democratic tradition. Jonathan Larsen embarked on a systematic effort to centralize authority, relying on a small, loyal band of top editorial managers to carry out his decisions and limiting the control of individual writers and editors over the pieces they worked on. He was also determined to rationalize office time and space, ending the crazy quilt of individual arrangements that left computer terminals idle before eleven A.M. and most of Tuesday (the day after the paper went to press) while they became the object of fierce competition at more popular times.

The *Voice*'s content underwent parallel changes. The paper was rigidly divided into sections devoted to particular kinds of stories. As a result, there was no more room for the uncategorizable, serendipitous piece of great writing or idiosyncratic weirdness that had once been a *Voice* specialty. There was also less and less room for genuine thought. Even in its best days, the *Voice* had never truly transcended the conventional journalistic values whereby reporting was considered both more important and harder work than essay writing or criticism. *Voice* reporters were generally rewarded with higher pay and more prominence in the paper: there was the front of the book, which was supposed to be news, and the back of the book (or the bus) with the cultural sections. Still, this distinction was regularly violated, and major staff freakouts could often be traced to a story on the arts or cultural politics that had made it onto the front page, scandalizing the "white boys." (There was, for instance, C. Carr's cover piece on the then obscure Karen Finley, which included graphic descriptions of her act and inspired an outraged column by Pete Hamill, months of letters to the editor, graffiti wars in the restrooms, and endless jokes about yams and where you could stuff them.)

Now the increasing balkanization of the paper, along with Larsen's own anti-intellectual bent, shored up the conventional mind-set. Once, my proposed headline for a cover story I'd edited was rejected because "it sounds as if the piece is an essay"—evidently something to be avoided at all cost. Cultural politics didn't go away, but like everything else it was institutionalized and ghettoized. On Larsen's watch the paper that had been home base for the most radical and iconoclastic feminist voices instituted a column called "Female Troubles," as well as columns for various ethnic groups. On the other hand, to my great puzzlement one indubitably good thing did happen during Larsen's editorship—the flowering of a lively and diverse group of black writers. My admittedly jaundiced theory was that Jon was so eager to enhance his liberal credentials with black bylines that he printed interesting stuff by black writers he wouldn't have accepted from white writers.

While individuals resisted the process of corporatization, it went forward without the concerted protest it would once have provoked. Though the *Voice* was still a highly profitable business—which is to say that the new regime was motivated more by ideology than by bottom-line concerns—changes in the surrounding economic and social environment had finally eroded the paper's internal culture of opposition. The cost of living had risen while opportunities in journalism had shrunk, especially opportunities for paying jobs at publications that featured serious writing, left politics, or any sort of "alternative" outlook (the *Voice*'s last serious competitor, the weekly *Soho News*, had folded several years earlier). The ethos of austerity and the celebration of corporate values had permeated the culture for a decade or more. A younger generation of *Voice* writers and editors had grown up under these conditions. Not only were their economic prospects far dicier than ours had been, their character formation was different: however "progressive" their politics or bohemian their cultural proclivities, many of them lacked the self-confidence (or arrogance), visceral antiauthoritarian impulse, and faith in the efficacy of collective action that were second nature to those of us imprinted with the '60s.

It did not take long for my relationship with Larsen to devolve into total war. I had been on a leave of absence when he arrived; when I came back I found that my "office" (which like most *Voice* offices was actually a small cubicle) had been allotted to someone else. I kept pestering the managing editor to give me my office back or assign me a new one, till she finally admitted that the boss didn't think I needed the space because "You're not here all the time." It seemed that when I *was* there I was expected simply to tote my stuff around, using whatever space was vacant, and doing without such amenities as my own telephone extension, let alone a terminal. I filed a grievance with the union, since our contract did not permit management to unilaterally change our working conditions. Having won my point and inspected my new cubicle, I assured Jon, "It will be fine — all it needs is a window and a carpet." His face registered a split second of panic before he realized I was joking — a moment that foreshadowed an unbridgeable sensibility gap.

After innumerable clashes with Larsen — who respected neither my ideas, the traditional autonomy I had exercised over the projects I supervised, nor the established boundaries of my job (which had allowed me to concentrate on my areas of interest and expertise) — I knew I had to get out of there. The question was how, in the age of austerity, I could get what I needed — a job that fit my skills, was reasonably engaging, was not morally offensive, and offered a decent income plus a modicum of freedom to do the writing I wanted to do. So far as I could see, there were no suitable possibilities in journalism: I already had the best job available to someone of my inclinations, and it wasn't good enough. Book publishing looked equally unappealing (though I did consider starting a freelance editing and editorial consulting business;

perhaps there was a market for the Maxwell Perkins figure publishing houses had long since dispensed with).

The alternative was the university: I had no advanced degrees, but perhaps with my credentials as a writer, an editor, and a feminist I could teach journalism or women's studies. The more I thought about it, the more I saw the academy—which I'd rejected nearly thirty years ago when I dropped out of graduate school—as my best shot. Whatever the realities at particular schools (and living with a professor, I knew a bit about those realities), at least in principle the university was an institution that supported the life of the mind, that considered one's "real work" part of one's job. In my experience, it was easier to maneuver by demanding that bosses live up to their professed principles than by insisting on principles they'd repudiated or never had in the first place.

In 1990 I left the *Voice* and joined the journalism faculty at New York University (of which more later). By my lights, the paper—which I continued to read assiduously, as if I were keeping a fever chart—became steadily duller and less influential. Its articles weren't talked about; hardly anyone I knew read it anymore. Apparently this defection was not limited to my friends; the *Voice*'s circulation dropped, even as costs, especially the cost of paper, were rising. By 1994 alarms were going off: although the *Voice* was still making money, it was increasingly marginal to the public conversation, widely regarded as the mouthpiece of a tired, outdated leftism at a time when conservatism and free-market libertarianism were hip. For the first time in years, the paper found itself pressed hard by competitors, the *New York Press* and *Time Out* (both offered extensive listings of cultural events; neither bore the leftist stigma). Jon Larsen quit or was fired. And then David Schneiderman did something that amazed and delighted me: he hired Karen Durbin as editor-in-chief.

Durbin was a cultural radical, a visceral democrat, pas-

sionate about ideas, a champion of the individual writer's
voice. She had been nurtured on the *Voice*'s oppositional culture, having first become a *Voice* writer, and then an editor, in
the early '70s. She was arts editor when Larsen was hired;
when she saw that he had no intention of allowing her any
power, she had left to be arts editor at *Mirabella*. She was
also a longtime close friend of mine, and I felt much the way
the FOBs must have done when their man ascended to the
White House. I was ensconced at NYU and didn't want a staff
job, but I accepted with gusto the offer of a column on media.
It seemed to be one of those rare moments of vindication:
evidently, Stern and Schneiderman had realized that corpo-
ratizing was not only bad for journalism, but bad for business,
and were ready to try letting the *Voice* be the *Voice*. Two-and-
a-half years later Durbin was gone, and so was I.

Score another for the culture of austerity. Larsen had de-
stroyed the old *Voice* culture and left a timid, unimaginative
bureaucracy in its place. There was no way one person could
substantially change this without wholehearted support
from management—especially the financial kind. Revitaliz-
ing the paper would have taken a huge investment in new
writers and editors and an equally substantial outlay for firing
people humanely, either by giving them large severance pack-
ages or keeping them on till they found other jobs (a necessity
not only for ethical reasons, but to forestall a debilitating atmosphere of panic in the office). And then, having made big
changes, management would have had to launch an expensive
promotional campaign to make sure the public knew about
them. But Stern, in *echt*-'90s fashion, was determined to cut
costs, a resolve that was reinforced by a steep rise in the price
of newsprint shortly after Durbin was hired. As a result, the
Voice became a reverse roach motel—you could get out, but
you couldn't get in. Durbin undertook a few highly publicized
firings and faced down the inevitable controversy, only to be

handed an ever-shrinking budget for new hires. Schneiderman also micromanaged the editorial budget in a way
that repeatedly undercut Durbin's authority. The double
whammy of hand tying and cost cutting was crippling. The
Voice did improve, but not enough. And though circulation
rose — especially after the paper instituted free distribution in
Manhattan — the paper's aggressive competition kept its ad
rates down, encouraging Stern to stick with his disastrous
penny-wise strategy.

After Durbin's departure, Schneiderman strongly intimated that he wanted a young editor, on the assumption that
such a person would attract a young readership, and his first
offer went to Michael Hirschorn of *New York* magazine. But
when Hirschorn didn't bite, he hired Don Forst, the former
editor of *New York Newsday,* a sixty-four-year-old with a classic
newsman's sensibility. Clearly the *Voice* has suffered a massive
identity crisis: the Larsen-Durbin-Hirschorn-Forst trajectory evokes the image of a drunk lurching from one direction
to another with only the vaguest idea of a destination. The
glib explanation is that the *Voice*'s historic identity as the cultural left's newspaper of record is no longer commercially viable in a conservative climate, but I don't think that's the real
issue. In New York there is still a sizable base of readers for
such a publication — a base that eroded in the first place not
because the *Voice* was too left-wing, but because it was too
boring. Besides, I believe that if you publish a paper that's
lively, iconoclastic, well written, and full of stories that can't
be found elsewhere, people will read it even if they hate your
politics — and that includes a lot of those panted-after young
people, especially the ones who are drawn to the libertarian
right not because they think Hayek was a genius but because
they want to be where the energy is.

Anyway, the *Voice* in its shakiest moments has never been
in danger of losing money. It's just that a *Village Voice* chas-

tened by the new economic order and out of sync with cultural-political fashion can't be expected to *roll* in money, as it did when it was riding the economic boom and the counter-cultural wave. It's hardly surprising that a businessman with no personal stake in the matter would be reluctant to accept less profit for the sake of preserving the paper as an opposi-tional force — especially in an era when accepting less profit for any reason is regarded as effete if not downright perverse. Yet it would arguably have made good business sense to take advantage of the *Voice*'s distinctive character — which was, among other things, a marketing niche — to secure its core au-dience while appealing to others precisely by departing from the general trend to bland, editor-driven, and idea-free jour-nalism. Instead, the apparent strategy has been to move the paper toward that "mainstream" where the (relatively) mass readership and its concomitant ad rates reside. But this strat-egy inevitably poses the problem of why anyone should read a publication that's so much like everything else out there, it has no compelling reason to exist.

In quest of a solution to this dilemma, the *Voice* has inexo-rably transformed itself from an editorial vision seeking an audience to a marketing vehicle seeking a formula. Its feature articles are conspicuously shorter, simpler, and dumber, with that *Voice* signature, the first-person essay, purged in favor of conventional news reporting. But perhaps Forst's most sym-bolically resonant act was to get rid of Jules Feiffer, whose car-toons bore something of the same relation to the *Voice*'s per-sona as Eustace Tilley to the *New Yorker*'s, by informing him that the *Voice* would be happy to continue to publish his work — it just didn't want to pay his salary. Increasingly, the paper has taken on the denatured flavor of the glorified pen-nysavers that mostly pass for an "alternative press" these days. The irony, of course, is that the *Voice* was the original model for all its canned versions: imitating them, it has become a simulacrum of itself.

Meanwhile, Leonard Stern has acquired several alternative weeklies and designed suburban versions of the *Voice* for Orange County and Long Island. In the context of these purchases, management announced the imposition of a new contract that forces *Voice* freelancers to give up most rights to their work; among other things it allows pieces to be recycled to all the papers in Stern's chain. This was an open break with the *Voice*'s pro-writer tradition. Yet compared to the spontaneous outrage that would once have greeted such a move, an anticontract organizing campaign by the National Writers Union went nowhere; nor did the *Voice*'s own union make any significant fuss. Many of the freelancers affected must have sensed that the game is up, that once the individual voice has been radically devalued, so has the source of their power. In effect, they are becoming anonymous content providers, nearly as interchangeable as classified-ad takers. And if their jobs can't be exported to Bangladesh, there is always the army of hungry would-be freelancers—the ones who still imagine their individual voices matter, and for whom solidarity's just another word for nothing left to lose.

As I write this, I'm on break from my classes at NYU, finally getting the block of time I need to finish an essay I've been working into the interstices of my schedule. My present life in the academy is, as the hounds of austerity view it, scandalously privileged. I teach three courses a year and, in lieu of a fourth course, direct a concentration in the journalism department's M. A. program. I have tenure. I have spring break, winter break, and those "three big reasons for becoming a professor"—June, July, and August. I'm about to spend a yearlong sabbatical, at three-quarters pay, working on a book. I have considerable control over my courses, my working hours, and the administration of my program. My salary and benefits are better than they were at the *Voice*, and my family and I live in affordable, if cramped, faculty housing (back in the Village, after all these years!). I am one of a shrinking minority of academics who enjoy such working conditions, which in my view are not pampered but merely humane.

When professors defend their perquisites, they like to invoke the special nature of their work: tenure is not about job security (perish the thought) but about academic freedom; summers off and sabbaticals are not vacations but a recharging of intellectual batteries; and so on. This line of argument not only incites the hounds all the more, since they think our work is a boondoggle to begin with, but reveals the extent to which they've colonized our minds. The truth is that in a rich postindustrial economy like ours, everyone should have job, or more to the point income, security; everyone should be able to speak their mind without being fired; and everyone should have time off to recharge their intellectual batteries, their sexual batteries, or any batteries they like. The university isn't Shangri-La; it's (for some of us) a decent workplace in a time when indecent is the norm.

On balance, academia has served my purposes well — or as well as I can reasonably expect at this unpropitious moment. Yet it has also subverted those purposes by plunging me into the kind of entangling institutional alliance I always tried so hard to avoid. In the first place, the classroom consumes much more of my energy than I naively imagined it would: unlike editing, which I experienced as a relief from the psychic demands of writing — an intellectual game of sorts — teaching makes intense demands of its own. It soon became important to me to teach courses that reflected my intellectual obsessions, and to have students who shared them — so I started a new concentration, which made me an administrator, involved me in department politics, led me to sit on certain

committees and plot how to raise money. The voice of austerity at NYU tends to whisper of future problems rather than
proclaim crises, but in one respect it's very loud: if faculty
want their projects to prosper, they had better be entrepre-
neurial. In June I'll dive into my book, but for now I have a
proposal I'd like you to read. . . . For me, the sabbatical that
lies ahead is at once a great gift and a great paradox: for a year it
will give me back what used to be my life. Imagine an antelope
transported from the African veldt to a lovingly constructed,
meticulously detailed simulated habitat in a state-of-the-art
zoo, while the hounds growl that in an age of austerity, a cage
should be enough.

VI

Their Libertarianism — and Ours

Those of us who call ourselves left libertarians feel pretty lonely these days. While the very word "libertarian" has become a synonym for "radical free-marketeer," the mainstream of the American left—defined broadly as the party of economic and social equality—seems content to cede both the word and the concept to the right. At best the contemporary left, with few exceptions, defends particular liberties and challenges particular repressive laws and policies while ignoring the structures of unfreedom built into institutions like the state, the corporation, the family, and the church. At worst it attacks "excessive" liberty as a mere extension of capitalist individualism, an offense to communal values, and/or a rationale for maintaining the position of dominant social groups. Most leftists are uncritically statist, merely complaining that the government is controlled by the wrong people and doesn't do enough of the right things. And though the left of course wants to redistribute corporate profits to workers, it shows little interest in attacking the authoritarian structure of the workplace or the puritanical assumptions of the work ethic.

Except for a few nanoseconds during the '60s, individual

freedom has always been a hard sell on the left. But in the embattled, dike-plugging, circle-the-wagons present, dissident voices are ever fewer and fainter. Even as the state becomes steadily more impotent and subservient to transnational capital, leftists are concentrating most of their meager energy on struggling to enlist state power in their behalf, whether to defend social welfare programs and affirmative action or to punish racist and sexist behavior. All too often, the soundtrack to this agenda consists of a whiny lecture about selfishness, meanness, and greed versus compassion, decency, and justice, as if America's problem were moral deficiency, rather than a declining standard of living or an increasingly repressive culture, and the solution were getting government to pull up our collective socks.

It's no wonder that the public prefers the right's language of freedom. Conservatives' distaste for government and for ideological curbs on free expression may be selectively applied, their celebration of free enterprise a rationale for ruthless class warfare, yet they speak to Americans' deepening feelings of entrapment and suppression in a way the left refuses or doesn't know how to do. Ironically, many leftists are all too eager to pander to the socially conservative values they imagine (erroneously) are the key to majority support, while dismissing libertarianism out of hand, despite its wide appeal. In reality, I'm convinced, the left has no hope of seriously influencing the public conversation unless it counters the right's conception of liberty with its own compelling vision of a free society.

Two recent books provide a good launching point for this argument: *Libertarianism: A Primer*, by David Boaz, executive vice president of the right-libertarian Cato Institute, and *What It Means to Be a Libertarian: A Personal Interpretation*, by Charles Murray, who needs no introduction. Together they do a fair job of articulating the dominant themes of right-wing antistatism. Boaz attempts a broad overview of libertarian philosophy, which he defines as a strict construction of classical liberalism based on a few first principles: individuals have the inalienable right to live as they choose so long as they respect the equal rights of others; property rights are the foundation of freedom and must not be abridged; "free markets are the economic system of free individuals"; government's role should be limited to prohibiting force and fraud, enforcing contracts, and providing for the national defense.

Murray is also a staunch advocate of minimal government, untrammeled property rights, and free-market economics (if slightly more willing than Boaz to allow exceptions for a limited number of public goods). He devotes the meat of his book to statistics purporting to show that every social improvement government has supposedly made would have happened anyway, and to "thought experiments" detailing how his proposals for economic deregulation, abolition of antidiscrimination laws, and so on might actually work. But he only reluctantly adopts the libertarian label—he would rather call himself a liberal, had the word not been appropriated by proponents of "an expansive government and the welfare state"—and indeed it hardly jibes with his professed admiration for Edmund Burke and his communitarian belief in "the indispensable roles that tradition and the classical virtues play in civic life."

Unlike Boaz, who genuinely seems to believe in civil liberties for dissidents and minorities, Murray basically defines freedom as the right of the conformist ("an ordinary human being making an honest living and minding his own business") to be left alone. He is especially concerned that landlords, employers, families, and other private parties not be deprived of "freedom of association" (i.e., freedom to discriminate) and its corollary, freedom to enforce social and moral norms without state interference. For Murray, the absolute

right of property owners to exclude from their premises anyone they find objectionable is the community's best defense
against drugs, pornography, and other "obnoxious" practices. His main quarrel with government is its propensity to
overrule traditional structures of authority in favor of individual rights and, worse, undermine those structures with
welfare programs that allow unwed mothers and other such
delinquents to survive. Like Boaz, he endorses "freedom of
personal behavior" in the absence of force or fraud. But while
this freedom comes first on Boaz's list, Murray mentions it
last, on the grounds that it's of little practical consequence,
since few people actually aspire to take advantage of it by testing social limits. (And if they did, in Murray's utopia, their
parents, neighbors, landlords, and bosses, unimpeded by
state-mandated tolerance or state subsidies for "irresponsible" behavior, would soon set them straight.)

In the end, though, these differences are more rhetorical
than real. Both authors subscribe to the fundamental fallacy
of right libertarianism, that the state is the only source of coercive power. Neither recognizes (surprise!) that the corporations that control most economic resources, and therefore
most people's access to the necessities of life, have far more
power than government to dictate our behavior and the day-
to-day terms of our existence. (Murray's claim that "if your
personal life were as closely monitored and regulated as the
vocational life of millions of Americans, you would rightly
consider it oppression" is unassailable, except that he means
government health and safety rules, not employers' decrees
about when you can go to the bathroom.) They show no sign
of noticing that a handful of global conglomerates exercises a
controlling influence on investment priorities, wages, interest rates, and conditions for workers and smaller businesses
around the world; or that these same corporate dogs routinely
wag the state tail, financing politicians who do their bidding

on economic and foreign policy while threatening to withhold credit and move jobs from any community (or country)
deemed insufficiently compliant.

Nor do Boaz and Murray acknowledge the ways corporate
control of mass media and cultural production limits the circulation of dissenting ideas and encourages patterns of de
facto censorship, like chain stores' refusal to stock unedited
CDs. (On the contrary, Boaz has the nerve to complain about
"court intellectuals" of the left whose big-government ideology is suborned by their patrons, such powerful dispensers of
Leviathan's largesse as . . . state universities and the National
Endowment for the Humanities! Now, who did you say funds
the Cato Institute? Santa Claus, right?) In fact, in three hun-
dred pages Boaz never mentions corporate power even to de-
bunk the idea, while Murray declares bluntly that economic
coercion does not exist, except, perhaps, in rare cases of "natural monopoly." The world as depicted in these books is the
projection of an imagination stuck somewhere in the eigh-
teenth century, its inhabitants myriad individual producers,
entrepreneurs, and workers all playing by the same rules,
freely competing and contracting in the marketplace. As Boaz
puts it, "If I trade my labor for a paycheck from Microsoft, it's
because I value the money more than the time, and the shareholders of Microsoft value my labor more than the money they
give up." And if we can't agree on how much of the shareholders' money my time and labor are worth? Well, gee, surely I
have as much choice of more obliging employers as Microsoft
has of less demanding workers.

The authors' discussion of property is equally simplistic.
In both books, the freedom to use land and other resources
for productive purposes, and the need for nonviolent means
of deciding who gets to use what, are conflated with ownership, defined by Boaz as the right to "use, control, or dispose

of an object or entity." But use is one thing, control and disposition another, and the elision of this distinction has no basis other than dogma. Not only have some societies managed quite well without individual ownership of land—various Native American tribes come to mind—but given that the earth and its resources were here before any of us, making the notion of literal ownership absurd, there is no defensible reason why those who first acquired property (usually through one or another form of conquest, not, as Boaz seems to think, by homesteading) should control its use by future generations.

Nor is having the personal use of resources the same as controlling and disposing of them for a profit. Boaz worries about someone coming along and confiscating "the wealth we've created"; but the more wealth property owners create, the less likely they are to have done it by themselves. Should they retain absolute control over resources that others—the propertyless with only their labor to sell—have helped produce? What happens to the latter's freedom under such a regime? Ignoring such obvious questions, the authors in effect reduce the issue of property to whether someone can (Murray's example) "come in off the street and walk off with your television."

Like Murray, Boaz upholds the right of property owners to discriminate against anyone whose values, appearance, or behavior they don't like; the impact on the freedom of those forced to conform to get a job or apartment—let alone those with the wrong skin color or other immutable trait—is not considered. Just as all economic dealings in Laissezfaire-world are purely voluntary transactions among equals, the moral and cultural judgments that inform those dealings are assumed to reflect millions of individual tastes and prejudices rather than ubiquitous social patterns like racism, homophobia, antidrug hysteria, and the like. Your employer says take a drug test or be fired? Find one who likes potheads. Turned down by a landlord who won't rent to blacks? No problem—the one down the block won't rent to white people.

There would seem to be a contradiction between this picture of happy pluralism and Murray's promotion of discrimination as a weapon against vice. But then, it seems that in every respect the freewheeling economic and cultural marketplace turns out to be a repository of stern, small-town bourgeois virtues. Indeed, both authors regard as a major selling point the claim that liberating our society from the heavy hand of the state would restore it to moral health: the undeserving poor would no longer have a claim on the earnings of the productive and diligent; the demise of social security and Medicare would revive thrift, prudence, and filial obligation to aging parents; without the cushion of welfare, unmarried childbearing would once again be socially stigmatized and economically punishing.

For Murray, of course, restoring what he forthrightly refers to as "social control" is the whole point of the antistatist agenda. Boaz, on the other hand, does note that some might consider this objective at odds with the libertarian aim of emancipating the individual. But he quickly disposes of this cavil. Libertarianism, he explains, aims to free the individual "from artificial, coercive restraints on his actions," not "from the reality of the world." Taxes, in other words, are artificial and coercive, but the constraints of Victorian morality are natural limits, like death.

From this perspective it's irrelevant that, say, collectivizing support of the "unproductive" old, while coercive in one respect, is liberating in others—allowing old people to live independently rather than with bossy or resentful children, enabling young people to take up acting or travel down the Amazon rather than thriftily, prudently going straight from school to planning for their retirement. The issue as Boaz presents it is not one set of social arrangements versus another, each with its own trade-off of freedom and restriction, but arrangements that uphold versus those that violate the natural order. It follows that except for physical violence, all nongovernmental restrictions on freedom—not only control of behavior through material reward and punishment but such age-old methods of social discipline as ostracism, humiliation, and psychological intimidation—are simply "reality" and off-limits to discussion.

Nonetheless, contradictions keep intruding on Boaz's polemic like the return of the repressed, especially when he tries to square liberty with family values. He supports equal legal rights for women and gays, opposes state policing of sexuality, and not only thinks the government has no business prohibiting gay marriage but argues—this is the high point of the book, as far as I'm concerned—that government should get out of the marriage business altogether, allowing marriage to become a voluntary contract like any other. Yet he naively sees the family as a "natural" association rather than a social institution—one that serves certain basic needs, to be sure, but is also chiefly responsible for enforcing male supremacy and sexual conformity (and for enlisting the state in these endeavors).

Boaz complains of unmarried welfare mothers' "long-term dependency" on government, as if it were unquestionably preferable that mothers be forced into long-term dependency on husbands. He seems unaware (perhaps he's too young to remember) that the stigma against unwed childbearing reinforced women's economic dependence, perpetuated a sexual double standard, and trapped countless people in miserable marriages; or that feminism, not welfare, is mainly responsible for its decline. He agrees that "women should have the right to work," yet laments that government benefits have "usurped responsibility for infants, children, and the elderly" formerly assumed by "the family"—for which read "housewives." (In any case, it will be news to most parents that government-provided day care is taking over child rearing.)

But never mind. If these purported libertarians are a waste of time for anyone trying to understand economic or social domination, surely they offer some insight into their chief target, the state? Strike three! Again, their basic axiom, that the state is a foreign body intruding on a free and independent marketplace, is firmly rooted in fantasy. In reality, the modern state came into being to serve the needs of the market: it backs that most elementary requirement for the free flow of capital, a reliable currency; builds the roads essential to moving goods; maintains the military and diplomatic umbrella that protects overseas investment and trade; and if necessary goes to war in behalf of those interests. And since the risk and instability built into capitalism—its "creative destruction"—is ultimately intolerable to the capitalists themselves, it is chiefly big business that has pressed the state to regulate markets, limit competition, and subsidize their costs with public funds. Even in this heady age of devolution, I have yet to hear the *Wall Street Journal* propose abolishing the Federal Reserve Board, with its dubious power to curb "inflation" (i.e., higher wages).

Until recently, the "big government" the free-marketeers want to dismantle had the active support of the American corporate elite. In the post–World War II era, business, government, and the labor movement forged a historic compromise for the avowed purpose of saving a capitalist system shaken by the crisis of the Depression, the power of the Soviet Union, and the threat of domestic and foreign radicalism. The deal was that economic regulation and cooperation between business and labor would ensure high wages and employee benefits, securing the loyalty—and the buying power—of a prosperous middle class; government's social welfare programs would provide a safety net for the old and poor; and the state, aggressively pursuing the cold war, would pour billions of federal military dollars into the private economy. In addition, business would profit by adapting to civilian use technologies originally developed for the military, like jet planes, plastics, and computers. Ignoring all this, Murray argues, as evidence that government programs make no difference, that "the trendline shows a regular drop in poverty from World War II through the 1960s," and that "the steepest drop in poverty occurred during the 1950s"—not during Johnson's War on Poverty. Whatever the accuracy of this controversial statistic, the fact is that the entire postwar period, the most prosperous in our history, was also the high point of state "interference" in the market.

But now business wants out of the deal, or anyway those parts of it that maintained Americans' standard of living. High wages and high taxes are obstacles to competition in the world market, while the demise of the Soviet regime and the paralysis of the left have removed any need to show that "capitalism delivers the goods." Yet already there's an incipient global infrastructure of regulation, in the form of institutions like the World Bank and International Monetary Fund, treaties like GATT and NAFTA, and the European Economic Community. And the pressure for more controls is likely to grow in the face of instability—indeed, near anarchy—in the former Soviet Union, as well as the spread of militant nationalism, fundamentalism, and other varieties of resistance to the new economic order.

At present, however, the power of transnational corporations has merely made it impossible for supposedly democratic governments to do anything. No matter who gets elected, politicians face the same demand: deregulate, reduce taxes, and enforce austerity on pain of disinvestment and a bad credit rating. The result is a flattening out of debate and a trivialization of politics that have fed the widespread, disgusted perception that all government does is throw our money down the drain. Meanwhile, for at least two decades moral conservatives of both the right and the left have carried on a totalitarian antidrug crusade and a relentless campaign against every form of "freedom of personal behavior," from abortion and divorce to the production and consumption of sexually dissident art and "unwholesome" popular culture to teenage sex and flirting in the office. In this cramped, guilt-ridden social atmosphere, right libertarianism has flourished, tapping people's frustration with politics and encouraging them to direct their thwarted impulses toward freedom into the narrow channels of freedom from taxes, freedom from "political correctness," freedom to resent the poor, freedom to discriminate, freedom to dream of sharing in the bounty of capitalist expansion.

There's a scary contrast between the emotional appeal of the libertarian right and the poverty of its thought. In part, the thinness of Boaz's and Murray's arguments can be attributed to what might be called vulgar anti-Marxism. The shared premise of their books—explicit in Boaz's dismissal of Marx as a proponent of "crabbed, reactionary statism" and his assurance that state meddling in the "natural harmony" of the free market is the sole cause of group conflict, implicit in both books' failure to note, let alone debate, the most basic socialist objections to liberal ideology—is that the collapse of Communism means Marx's monumental critique of capitalism can be safely ignored. While this is no doubt a sound political judgment, it's an intellectual disaster. Among other things, making class antagonism the great unmentionable precludes any insight into why, if classical liberalism is so terrific, it was supplanted in the first place. Boaz does make a brief stab at this question, concluding that the main culprit was historical

amnesia: people took for granted the "unprecedented improvement in living standards" the Industrial Revolution had
wrought and didn't realize how much better off they were than
past generations. "Charles Dickens," he complains in one of
his sillier moments, "bemoaned the already waning practice
of child labor that kept alive many children who in earlier eras
would have died."

Equally disabling is the authors' resolutely pre-Freudian
mentality. Boaz is an Aristotelian rationalist, while Murray
leavens his faith in reason with loyalty to "tradition and the
nonrational aspects of the human spirit." But both see human motivation as entirely conscious, deliberate, and self-
interested, or as Murray puts it, "absent physical coercion,
everyone's mind is under his own control." Here too they are
in sync with contemporary political fashion, which is as
contemptuous of psychoanalysis as of Marxism. Yet with no
recognition of unconscious conflict between desire and fear,
the origins of that conflict in the unequal struggle of the
pleasure-seeking infant with parental authority, and conscience as its uneasy resolution, it's impossible to see morality
for what it is — a structure of internalized coercion. This is not
to say that all moral imperatives are oppressive, any more than
all laws are; only that morals are no less socially imposed than
laws, and should be no less subject to examination and criticism. Since Boaz and Murray do not understand this, they
have no use for — indeed no conception of — questions I consider essential to the project of human freedom: Do "family
values" produce socially submissive, sexually frustrated people whose unconscious rage, mixed with guilt, surfaces as aggressive moralism? Do we glorify constant work and look with
suspicion on idleness because we need to, even in a world
where technology is increasingly severing the link between
productivity and human labor? Or are we punishing our-

selves for guilty desires—and are we therefore less likely to question the conditions of our work, and whose purposes it serves?

The authors are of course equally unreflective about the psychosocial implications of their own worldview. They both argue, for instance, that the basis of our natural right to freedom is "self-ownership." This is a curiously alienated idea: I don't "own" myself, as if it were an object somehow separable from my subjectivity; I *am* myself. But it makes sense as a reaction to the experience of having your body and psyche controlled by others. If you can't overcome the split between your deepest desires and the socialized self your upbringing has forced you to adopt, you can at least assert your control over "it"—at the same time denying your earliest and most profound loss of autonomy by fixating on the state as your only antagonist in the struggle for control. (Is it entirely fortuitous that right libertarians are so fond of parental metaphors for government? Boaz: "Conservatives want to be your daddy, telling you what to do and what not to do. Liberals want to be your mommy, feeding you, tucking you in, and wiping your nose.") The right to property, in turn, becomes a means of extending control to your surroundings; but since control is only a substitute for genuine satisfaction, you can never have enough of it.

Boaz unwittingly touches on this truth when he argues that we need property because scarcity is inherent in the human condition: our unlimited wants will always outstrip our finite resources. It doesn't occur to him that forbidden, unspeakable wishes for real emotional and erotic freedom may stubbornly press for expression in the socially acceptable guise of "insatiable" material desires. This dynamic suggests why Boaz and Murray can see no serious distinction between limiting corporate control of land or capital and borrowing someone's toothbrush without permission. In the right-libertarian unconscious, the very definition of free-dom becomes control, expansion, and domination — in other words, the will to power.

The story of the right's success has everything to do with the resonance of this definition for large numbers of Ameri-cans, up and down the class ladder. But idealists like Boaz (I'm not sure I can say the same for Murray) are unlikely to be pleased with the results. Under conditions of worsening eco-nomic inequality, the yearning for freedom-as-power is easily appropriated by right-wing populists and ultimately by fas-cists. Libertarian conservatives may abhor the Pat Buchanans and the paramilitary thugs; all the same, the right-libertarian mind-set has helped create them.

On the other hand, leftists have been unable to combat the right's conception of freedom, or offer an alternative, because for the most part they, too, unconsciously identify freedom with power. Unlike the right libertarians, however, they fear the destructive potential of the will to power and so conclude that individual freedom is inherently dangerous. Instead of rejecting the state "parent," they aspire to take over the role and suppress "selfishness" in the interest of "social justice." Where right libertarians see their moral agenda as natural and therefore compatible with freedom, leftists openly use guilt as a political weapon. Freedom becomes a positive value only when redefined to mean collective empowerment for subordinate classes and social groups.

Ironically, in seeking to curb the individual will to power in favor of equality, leftists invest their own subterranean de-sires for freedom-as-power in the activist state. In my view, the revival of the left depends on relinquishing this investment. We need to recognize that despite appearances the state is not our friend, that in the long run its erosion is an opportunity and a challenge, not a disaster. I don't want to be misunder-stood: I'm not suggesting that we stop supporting social secu-

rity or national health insurance or public schools or antidiscrimination laws. If my immediate choices are the barbarism
of unleashed capital or a state-funded public sector, the tyranny of uninhibited private bigotry or state-enforced civil
rights, I choose the state. Or rather, I choose the social goods
and civil liberties that are available under state auspices.

The distinction is important, because the idea that the
state *gives* us these benefits is a mystification. Basically, Murray is right: goverment does not cause social improvement. In
actual historical fact, every economic and social right that
we've achieved since the nineteenth century has been hard-
won by organized, militant, and often radical social movements: the labor movement; the socialist, communist, and an-
archist movements; the new left student movement; the black
and feminist and gay liberation movements; the ecology
movement. (Such movements are yet another social force that
Boaz and Murray see no need to include in their analysis of the
individual versus the state—in part, I imagine, because the
left itself so often forgets their importance.) The role of the
state from the New Deal and the postwar compact till the start
of its present no-more-Mr.-Nice-Guy phase was to manage
potentially destabilizing social conflict by offering carefully
limited concessions to the troublemakers.

Since the liberal state's priority is stability, not equality
(let alone emancipation), those concessions generally took
shape as hierarchical, bureaucratic agencies designed more
to control their clients than to serve them. Nonetheless, their
existence succeeded in defusing the social movements, not
only because they represented real if partial victories, but because the government was able to take the credit and con-
vince the public—including most movement activists—that
nothing more was possible. From labor laws that restrict the
right to strike and define who can and can't be organized to
Nixon's strategy of affirmative action, which ignored systemic

racial inequality to focus on upward mobility for the black middle class, state social policy has never wavered in its primary allegiance to the corporate elite. The government's current rush to abandon any pretense of social responsibility ought to make this painfully clear: what the state supposedly giveth it promptly taketh away as soon as the balance of social power shifts. In this case, of course, social power is shifting away from the national state itself; liberals and social democrats are still trying to board a train that's already left the station.

In parallel fashion, the statism of the cultural left does not further equality so much as it reinforces law and order. Originally, the relation of the black, feminist, and gay movements to the state was adversarial: they demanded an end to state-sponsored discrimination, from Jim Crow and the body of family law codifying women's inferior status to the refusal of the criminal justice system to take lynching, rape, and wife beating seriously to the criminalization of abortion and homosexual sex. Such battles are of course still going on — for gays, especially, they are a major arena — but the emphasis has long since shifted to demanding that the state use its power to prohibit racist and sexist practices in the "private" realm. Insofar as the demand is to outlaw overt, provable discriminatory acts by employers, landlords, store owners, and so on, it simply aims for public recognition that (pace Boaz and Murray) discrimination is a coercive act as unacceptable as violence or theft. But the problem, from the social movements' point of view, is that overt, deliberate discrimination is only the crudest expression of a deeply rooted culture of inequality. For many opponents of that culture, it has seemed a logical next step to invoke state power against patterns of behavior that reinforce white male dominance and exclude, marginalize, or intimidate vulnerable groups.

Actually, it's a plunge into dangerous illusion. The ingrained behavior and attitudes that support the dominant culture are by definition widespread, reflexive, and experienced as normal and reasonable by the people who uphold them. They are also often unconscious or ambiguous. A serious effort to crush racism and sexism with the blunt instrument of law would be a project of totalitarian dimensions—and still it would fail. Transforming a culture and its consciousness requires a different kind of politics, a movement of people who consistently and publicly confront oppressive social patterns, explain what's wrong with them, and refuse to live by them—to stay in the closet, make dinner, smile, ignore the patronizing remark or the nervous surveillance. In fact, the turn toward the state is a symptom of the social movements' current weakness. It's the disappearance from public conversation of any ongoing critique of "normal," everyday sexism that makes women think the only way to fight male pressure to have sex they don't want is to prosecute it as rape. It's the general repressiveness of the social climate that encourages moves to ban offensive speech or define any form of sexual expression in the workplace as sexual harassment. The main effect of these maneuvers is to foment confusion, cynicism, and sexual witch-hunts, trivialize sexual violence, and legitimize conservative demands for censorship—while at the same time ceding the moral high ground of free expression to the right.

It's time for the left to become a movement again. That means, first of all, depending on no one's power but our own. It means formulating a vision of what kind of society we want and agitating for that vision, in every inventive way we can, wherever we find ourselves. It means challenging, at every opportunity and in every venue of our daily lives, the institutions, policies, practices, conventions, attitudes that oppose and repress our vision. It means creating alternative institutions and experimenting with new ways of living to figure out how our vision might work.

My own vision of what I want — of why I want a movement — has at its center the conviction that freedom and equality are symbiotic, not opposed. While it's unlikely that social coercion — governmental or otherwise — will ever be entirely surpassed, my measure of a good society is the extent to which it functions by voluntary cooperation among people with equal social and political power. For all their wrongheadedness, the right libertarians have grasped a couple of basic truths. One is that there is no such thing as a free society without free individuals. The other is that the interaction of free individuals produces what they call "spontaneous order" and what I would call self-government or simply democracy. What they don't understand is how much has to change to let free individuals and spontaneous order flourish. That's where we come in — or should.

ACKNOWLEDGMENTS

I thank the editors who assigned, critiqued, or otherwise facilitated the appearance in various publications of the original versions of these essays: Brian Morton, Robert Boyers, Michael Vazquez, Henry Finder, Henry Louis Gates Jr., Michael Lerner, Alice Chasin, Barry Gewen, Chris Lehmann, David Mehegan, Eric Alterman, Katha Pollitt, Richard Lingemann, Katrina vanden Heuvel, Stanley Aronowitz, Jonathan Cutler. I especially want to thank my editors at the *Village Voice*, Karen Durbin and Joe Wood, for their collaboration in the ongoing exchange of ideas on our cultural common sense that produced most of the sections of "Decade of Denial."

I thank Micah Kleit, my editor at Beacon, for his invaluable advice on how to focus this book and put it together, his steadfast commitment to the project, his encouragement and moral support. I am also grateful to Deborah Chasman of Beacon for her editorial suggestions.

I thank Charlotte Sheedy, my agent, for her work on my behalf and for being on my wavelength.

I want to express my debt to Stanley Aronowitz and our countless hours of breakfast and dinner-table conversation on politics, economics, and culture. In particular, Stanley's analysis of the labor movement has strongly influenced my conception of the relationship between economic and cultural issues.

Finally, my thanks to David Glenn for complaining, in an otherwise sympathetic review of my last book, that I didn't pay enough attention to class.